MW00412352

Unapologetically

FAVORED

COURTNEY KITTRELL

A woman
A leader
A testimony.

Unapologetically
FAVORED

gatekeeper press

Columbus, Ohio

Unapologetically Favored: A woman. A leader. A testimony.

Published by Gatekeeper Press
2167 Stringtown Rd, Suite 109
Columbus, OH 43123-2989
www.GatekeeperPress.com

ISBN (hardcover): 9781642377743
eISBN: 9781642377736

DEDICATION

This book is dedicated to every person who feels as if they are the "only one". The only one that has emotional issues, the only one who is going through depression, the only one who is not happy, the only one who has experienced a profound loss, the only one who wants to feel loved by their parents, the only one who has hit rock bottom and is ashamed to speak about it, the only one who has failed as a parent, a sibling, a spouse, a friend or leader, the only one who wants to be who they truly are, but too afraid of not being accepted, the only one afraid of being rejected by society, the only one traveling down life's path with fear of not knowing where the path is leading. You are not the only one!

We are all unique in our own way. No two things will ever be an exact match. No two lives will ever travel the same exact path. Your life is meant for you! The foundation was laid when you were born into this world. It is up to you to build the sidewalks, the homes, the stores, plant the trees, water the flowers, and welcome people along your journey. Your journey will not always be smooth or easy. There will come storms and rain. Buildings will collapse and some flowers might die along the way, but your journey will continue on. Re-build what is important to you; the homes and buildings representing your relationships with family and friends. Plant more flowers representing the beauty and the good you are leaving behind also it could be your legacy for others to follow. Make sure you continue to water and nurture everything so they can continue to grow throughout your life. Welcome those who genuinely care for you and want the best for you into your life. These will be the people that will give you a hand in building what you need to become successful. Talk to them, let them pour into you. Open your mind, your heart, and your eyes. These are the people who were meant for you, good or bad, to be a teacher, a blessing, or a lesson. When your skies start to darken, the thunder begins to clap, and the rain pours down, don't run and hide. Don't feel ashamed. Don't give up. You need water to survive. You need tough times to build resiliency and carry on through life. You need tough times to grow.

You will cross paths with others along this journey going through the same experience as you. Stop to talk to them. Give them a hand. Listen to their story and their pain. Be a healer by just smiling at them. Tell them, "It's going to be okay." You might come across a friend who has lost a loved one and you have as well. You are not the only one. Your next stop might lead you to a family member who is battling depression quietly with no one to lean on. You are battling the same thing. You are not the only one. Your final destination could lead you to the strongest leader in the world who is struggling with their confidence, their image, and their personal life and to this, you can also relate. You are not the only one. Stop living your life in silence. Stop walking around surrounded by fear, despair, loneliness, confusion, and the "I'm the only one" mentality. Speak up! You physical and mental health depend on you to take care of it.

I implore you to hold your head high, walk in confidence, find your purpose in life and own it. Accept who you are and love who you are. Your life has value and meaning. If you find a torn dollar bill on the ground, you can tape it back together and still spend it. That dollar never loses its value. When you can hit rock bottom and your life falls apart for a short period of time, when everything is mended back together you will still have value! Don't devalue yourself because of the scars and bruises that life has left on you.

Success is not a hand-out. It comes with minor set-backs and failures, but a set-back only means a major come back and its only failure when you fall and never rise up. I want you to know that you are not the only one.

CHAPTER ONE

Accidents Happen

"**G**wen, I know you're pregnant." My grand-mother, my father's mother, was a real character with impeccable manners and a sense of intuition. A heavyset woman with wide hips, big buttocks, and nicely manicured nails, she had light skin, and her cheeks were rosy and grew darker the more she became upset. Those hot flashes surely set the tone for our days. My grandmother never knew who her father was growing up, but we all assumed he was a white man because of her fine silky hair and fair skin. A well-to-do lady by African-American standards, she was never short on male suitors, but for some reason, they never stayed around long enough. My grandmother liked everything in its place, and there was a place for everything. She was living in a small two-bedroom apartment around the time my mother found out she was pregnant by my father, Charles.

"Anne, I am not pregnant. Why do you keep saying that?" My mother was easily annoyed by grandmother. She knew how to press an issue to be seen her way.

"Yes, you are! Look at you! Your face is getting full, and you're always tired. Every time we drive over that small hump on 16th Street, you get sick!"

My mother, Gwen, was a beautiful brown-skinned, short, and petite woman. She wore big glasses that slid off her nose when she looked down. Gwen had a broad smile that highlighted the dimple in her right cheek and the signature family gap between her two front teeth. She rocked her afro during the 1970s and soon started straightening her hair, keeping it in the latest styles. My mother was the life of every party. Dancing was her forte, and she was not shy in showing off her dance moves. Living her life to the fullest was also my mother's best quality. And because she could get down with the best of them, she was never short on male attention either. To get away from home, my mom enrolled in North Carolina A&T State University in Greensboro, North Carolina. Her move was the right course in her life for her at the time.

After living in different parts of the world because my grandfather served in the Army, the family finally retired and settled in Fayetteville, North Carolina. Greensboro wasn't too far, but far enough from Fayetteville that my grandparents were not going to show up for a surprise visit. During this time, my mother met my father through respective party friends. My parents hit it off right away.

"Well, I don't think I am pregnant!" My mother was annoyed by this time. My grandmother always had a way of "reading" people, and for some reason, she could tell what was going on with a person by the vibes she felt they gave off. My mom once said to me that she thought my grandmother dabbled in voodoo, but nothing was ever substantiated. My grandmother knew my mother was pregnant with me, but my mom didn't want to hear any of that reality even if it was true—especially coming from my grandmother. With having a child, it was not like you could pick and choose which days would work for you or fit in your schedule in caring for an infant, especially when you were used to doing what you wanted when you wanted—attending all the hottest basement parties and drinking. Young people want to get it in. Being pregnant meant facing the truth that she had been careless, and also that her life was about to unalterably change. Would she be able to finish college? Was my father going to be a man? Where would she go? How would her parents feel?

"I'm taking you to the clinic tomorrow when you get off work. I told you what would happen messing around with Charles. You know good and well he ain't in no position to want to settle down and raise a baby." My grandmother never held back punches. If something was messed up about you, she would tell you straight like it was. That was one thing I admired about her. She did not have a "fuck filter," meaning she did not give a fuck about how you felt when she talked to you.

"He out running these streets with his buddies. You think Charles is gonna stop his life for you?"

My dad was a handsome man; a high school football star, rich brown, with very thick, curly black hair. He stood

5'8 and weighed 185 pounds. Charles would wear his clothes tight enough to make the girls do a double take. He was a player and had females after him. Nothing was kept a secret in his pants. He maintained a well-trimmed mustache above his top lip that ran down evenly on both sides of his mouth. Charles was also the life of the party. You knew when my dad was around because his voice was deep, and it carried for miles on end, especially when he was laughing or cracking a joke about somebody. Even though he was the most popular man in the room, there was something about my mother that attracted him.

"Whatcha gonna do when the pregnancy test comes back positive?" my grandmother asked my mom.

"Anne, I don't know. I'll have to figure something out. I'm living with my co-worker right now. I know I can't stay there with a baby," my mother told my grandmother.

"Well, my daughter Phyliss is moving out soon. You and Charles can stay with me. I'll move into the small room with the twin beds. You and Charles can take my room with the full-sized bed."

"Anne, I don't want to be a burden. Let me figure this all out. Hell, I don't even know if I'm pregnant or not!"

The next day, after the visit to the clinic confirmed that my mother was indeed pregnant with me, her life changed, and as promised, my grandmother let my mom and dad move in with her. Trying to get organized, Charles and Gwen were forced to occupy the closet in the room where my grandmother slept, and my grandmother occupied the closet in my parents' room. This made for an awkward situation when my mother would dress for work in the morning. Having to creep into a different bedroom to gain access to your personal belongings was not precisely the domestic dream for my parents.

After a couple of days went by, while Anne was away from home with her boyfriend, my mom was finally fed up with the closet arrangements, so she took it upon herself to make life easy for everyone. One day, while at work, my mother received a phone call.

"Gwen, you have a phone call on line one." My mom was confused. Who was calling her work?

"Hello?" she said very passively, not knowing my grandmother was on the other end. Nothing could have prepared my mom for this one-way conversation.

"Who the hell gave you permission to go in my closet and move my things!" Anne was pissed.

"Anne! I was trying to help out and make it easy, so you didn't have to worry about switching closets! You were not home for the past couple of days so I figured you would not mind," my mom exclaimed.

"You don't touch nothing that belongs to me! You understand me?! Since you want to rearrange stuff so bad, you can rearrange yourself out my damn apartment!" My grandmother slammed down the phone.

I think my grandmother may have been a bit bipolar. One minute, she could charm the life out of you with her sweet and innocent voice. Then, in a split second, she would curse you out like a drunken sailor who just ran out of beer! Somedays, you never knew what you were going to get.

That evening, Charles picked up my mom from work. Still upset, my mother told him about the phone call she received from his mom. When they arrived home, Dad tried to unlock the door with the apartment key. The key would not budge. He flipped the key over and tried again—still nothing. My grandmother had changed the lock on the door. Upset, he broke a window pane to gain access to the apartment. Once he was in, my dad went directly to the bedroom and packed some clothing and shoes for himself and my mom. They left and stayed with friends until they could save enough money to move out on their own permanently—or at least that was the idea at the time. The day Mom told my dad she was pregnant with me, my dad's best friend, Wade "Stymie" McCormick, was hit and killed by a drunk driver. The night it happened, while at a party, Stymie had been outside talking to a young lady who was sitting in the driver's side of a car parked on the curb. The car door was open, and Stymie was in the squat position between the door and driver seat. Out of nowhere, a drunk driver hit Stymie and snatched off the car door. Stymie was pinned and dragged under the car, killing him. This event impacted my father to this day. My grandmother always said, "When the lord takes a life, he gives another." My father was not a permanent fixture in my life, and I often wondered whether when my dad looked at me, he saw his best friend. Was I too much for him? Was I a constant reminder of that fatal night? Perhaps that would explain why he has never been a consistent part of my life. Every single year, my dad wishes Stymie a happy birthday, yet I receive nothing for my birthdays or even Christmas. Gwen and Charles eventually broke up due to my dad's infidelity and unwillingness to be a father. My parents loved each other, but they were not IN LOVE with each other. Mom had to do what she had to do. With hardly any money, she moved out on her own and cared for me the best she could.

Gwen was back in the dating scene by the time I turned three years old. One day, while my mother was asleep, I took it upon myself to give her the best three-year-old's hairstyle I could imagine. I clipped in her hair every colorful, plastic hair barrette I could find. Suddenly, there was a knock at our door. Because we didn't have a lot of furniture at the time, the sound of the knock echoed off the walls of the apartment like the voices of a choir echo off the walls of a cathedral. My mom awakened from her sleep and jumped up. Feeling the barrettes slapping her in the face as she sat up, she knew I had been up to no good.

"Courtney! What in the world did you do?"

Gwen scrambled, trying to remove the rainbow assortment of bows from my three-year-old's braids. My mother looked like a black Pippi Longstocking, but she was still beautiful to me. Mom made her way to the door, still searching for lost barrettes in her hair. She opened the door slowly. On the other side, stood a 6'1, lean, handsome, fair-skinned gentleman, with long, black, wavy hair pulled into a tight ponytail, and hazel eyes. Mom still had a couple of lost hair barrettes in her hair when she opened the door. An explosion of laughter occurred.

"Excuse my hair. Courtney decided to play beauty salon while I was asleep," my mother said ruefully.

"It's okay," he replied. "She did a good job." His name was Michael Lee McClain, and he would be the father I never had.

CHAPTER TWO

Mike

ichael Lee McClain was my stepfather. He was twelve years older than my mother, but the age difference was never an issue. Mike grew up very poor with his five siblings in the mountains of Virginia. His mother was absent, so all six children were shuffled around to live with family members, who at the time could not afford to take in orphaned children. Some nights, they went hungry because there was not enough food to go around. When they did eat, they were forced to sit on the floor and not allowed at the table with their foster family. Mike's childhood was sad, but it made him and his siblings understand the meaning of taking care of a family.

As an adult, Mike was well known in Greensboro because he owned an automotive center called Mike's Tire on East Bessemer Avenue. Not long after my mother and Mike started dating, Gwen became pregnant with my brother. In 1984, Mike found out that his business was not doing well. His accountant was making errors with the finances, leaving the company to struggle. Facing the stress of not knowing if his business would fold and finding out that my mom was pregnant at the same time put Mike under a lot of pressure. In the spring of 1984, he had a stroke. Gwen was right there by his side. Mike never went back to work, and his automotive business closed permanently. To get his life back on track, Mike moved in with his Uncle Emory, who at the time, worked for United Taxi Company driving taxi cab #25. United Taxi employed my stepdad once he was able to work again. When Uncle Emory passed away, Mike was given his taxicab, and Mike drove the taxicab until the day he died.

Mike loved driving his taxi. It gave him the freedom he wanted, and it allowed him to be his own boss. He didn't have set hours but was very disciplined. Mike would leave the house every morning around nine o'clock and come home between 8:30-9:00 p.m. Once in the house, he'd empty his pockets, placing his wallet on the side table in the living room. Then, he would take a shower and put on a crisp, white V-neck T-shirt and a pair of light blue or dark blue corduroy shorts that looked very short because his legs were so long. Then he would make his nightly drink of Canadian Mist and Pepsi in an antique green drinking glass. He would grab his wallet and his bag of money he made that day and meticulously count every dime. He laid everything in stacks—all the ones together, fives together, tens together and so on. Mike then moved on to the loose change. Every night was clockwork, and nothing broke the cycle.

He rented two Blockbuster Video Store VHS tapes every night except Sundays. On Friday nights, it was always TGIF that included the hit sitcoms Full House and Family Matters. On Sundays, we watched In Living Color, and Roc followed by whatever Disney movie was premiering.

Due to his caring nature, Mike shared his love to those who couldn't take care of themselves. Driving his cab, he met a lot of people. His most memorable passenger was Ms. Lee, a 4'11, petite and fragile white lady. Her face was old, and she had many wrinkles. Her hair was silver, long, stringy and flowed down her back. Her nails were thick, yellow, and very long. The house Ms. Lee lived in seemed as if the bedroom, living room, and kitchen were all one room. It had an old, stale, mothball smell and was dark and gloomy. Mike adopted Ms. Lee as his mother. If she was sick, he picked her up from her home and took her to the doctor's office. When Ms. Lee needed groceries, he would buy them for her. Mike was the son Ms. Lee never had, and Ms. Lee was the mother he missed.

One day, after my baby brother was born, I went with Mike on his trip to check on Ms. Lee. We walked into her home, and she was excited to see him. He always brightened her days.

"Mike! Oh boy! Thank you for coming." She reached up to and gave him a hug with the signature old lady pat on the back.

"Hey, Miss Lee. How are you feeling today? I stopped by the store to bring you some things." He placed the plastic shopping bags on her kitchen table.

"Oh, I'm mad at the Meals-On-Wheels folks. They ain't been by here this week. They know I don't like making stuff to eat when I can get it for free! I have it on my mind to call the city!" Ms. Lee was plenty upset.

As the adults talked about adult stuff, I scanned the room. My eyes became fixated on an old dusty wooden shelf hanging on the wall. The shelf had 1,001 knick-knacks of random white porcelain figurines, greeting cards, dingy white doilies, and glass containers that contained dinner mint candy. In the center of it all, was a picture of my brother and only my brother. At that time, looking at my baby brother's picture alone on the shelf, I didn't know why that bothered me, but it did. That was the first time I felt like I was not my stepdad's child. I continued to scan the room, taking in all the dust on the picture frames hanging on the walls along with the couch that looked like it was wrapped in brown burlap material. The visit seemed like hours on hours to me as a kid, but we only visited with Ms. Lee for maybe thirty minutes.

"Okay, Ms. Lee. I have to get home. I will call and check on you later this week. If you need something, call me and let me know." He gave her a hug.

"I will, Mike. Thank you for stopping by. Don't nobody love me like you do. I sho' do 'preciate it. If the good lord is willing and the creek don't rise, I will see you soon!" Then, Mike and I left.

Mike had a daughter, Alice, from a previous marriage. Growing up, it always seemed to be a power struggle between the two. I can only attribute it to Mike not being in Alice's life as a father, but she still wanted the love and affection from her dad as I wanted from mine. So, I could relate to her emotionally. My mom was accepting of Alice, but dealing with a "baby mama" could not have been easy. Alice was just a teenager when she had her first baby, and I know that upset Mike to the point that, even though I was not biologically his, he was very strict with me. I felt like I was paying Alice's debts because he was not going to let me be another young black teenage mother. I was not going to be a statistic.

"You will not have any boys in this house! You understand me?" he shouted.

He would tell me this all the time, but my friends in the neighborhood were boys except my friend Shameka. She was my only female friend growing up. My best friend, Jay, lived up the street with his little brother Josh, who was my brother's best friend at the time, and their little sister Jaime. We were all very close. So, when Mike would tell me I couldn't have boys in the house, he was telling me, I couldn't have friends in the house. Well, that was how I heard it in my head at the time.

"I got it. Jeez! I can't wait to grow up and move out of this stupid house! I'm not a kid!"

I stormed away mad as hell like, "First of all, I don't even like boys like that! And you're not my dad, so you can't tell me what to do!" At the time, I had a lot of male friends. I attracted male attention, and they would flirt with me, but I was never interested in entertaining them. I played kickball in the street wearing a skirt and no shoes. I jumped creeks and watched the boys shoot squirrels out of the trees in my backyard. Me...and boys...getting together was not a thing at the time, and it never occurred to me why.

Hindsight is always 20/20. We never know what is meant by the actions of our parents until we are in a predicament where what they were yelling about comes around to bite us in the ass. There were times I wondered how my stepdad felt about raising another man's daughter. When my father would randomly show up and want to spend time with me, I knew Mike had a little bit of anger about it, but he would reluctantly agree to let me spend the day with my dad, knowing that Charles was going to excite me and then leave again. I wanted so badly to believe that each time my father came back into my life for one of his mini visits that he would finally stay forever.

"You know your father doesn't love you, right? If there was an option to leave you on the curb or pick up a woman, you would be sitting on the curb in the cold."

Those were Mike's exact words to me one evening as we sat in the living room watching television. To this day, I still don't know where that statement came from or how long he'd held that thought. As far as I was concerned, he was mean and disrespectful. How dare he talk about my dad like that when he didn't even know him, I thought. The words cut me deep. I felt abandoned, lost, and alone. Why did my dad not love or want me? My stepdad wasn't my real dad, so he couldn't love me like that. I figured that my real dad didn't love me either or else he would never have left me.

"Mike, don't tell that girl that!" Mom yelled. "What is wrong with you?"

At least she had my back, but still, what Mike said had meaning, truth, and substance. I wanted so badly to cry, but I controlled my emotions. What good would crying have done? Mike was telling the truth. He was the one raising me. My stepdad was my father. He was providing for my needs and sometimes my wants, but what I truly wanted was my dad. I wanted Charles Edward Kittrell, Jr. There was so much he was missing out on. I was playing the violin, the piano, and I loved to sing. I was in Girl Scouts, I was making A's and B's in school, and I was on the honor roll. I was an all-American girl, but he would never know. Would he ever come back into my life?

I respected Mike for accepting my mother and me. He did what he knew to do in raising me. It was never all easy, but I can't say it was terrible either. A stepparent relationship is the hardest relationship there is. Stepparents assume all duties and responsibilities of a biological parent. Some relationships are a success while some ultimately fail. The failure comes from the stepparent not knowing or understanding the child and not knowing how to communicate expectations and standards.

Expectations and standards should always be both ways in a "step" household. A stepparent cannot reasonably walk into a family and start demanding things and making decisions about the child or start regulating the child's life without getting to know the child. From the child's view, a stepparent is a stranger—no ifs, and, or buts about it. The same way a teacher has to gain the respect and loyalty of their students, or a manager of their workers, is the same way a stepparent has to develop trust and commitment from the child. Be patient, be understanding, be loyal to the child, and listen to how they feel. Know that they are scared of you because they don't know you.

Children know the feeling of being nurtured. They understand the feeling of love, and most times, what a child wants is love, understanding, compassion, trust, and an open dialogue with the stepparent. The stepparent, in turn, wants the same with the child. It is imperative that mutual discussion is tabled on both sides to have and maintain a healthy family relationship. Mike and I never had the opportunity to talk about his expectations of me. I simply assumed the traditional daughter role, and he understood the regular father role. A lack of communication led to our arguments and disagreements, leaving me feeling like I was not good enough because I was not his. Lack of communication also left me with little trust because I did not know his intentions regarding raising me. I would never get a chance to thank Mike for being stern with me and ensuring I was on the right path. He protected me from all harm, but I was too young to understand his reasoning. Mike would soon pass away and leave me with emotional voids I never knew existed until later in life.

CHAPTER THREE

My Brother's Keeper

Michael Lee McClain, Jr. was born October 23, 1984. He was very light, with big curly rings of hair covering his head. His bottom lip hung open, and he had a little drool. His smile was always half-cocked, making him look drunk. Michael was a good baby. I knew my stepfather was proud to have a son because he had only girls, Alice and me. My brother was his daddy's child. He could do no wrong.

It became apparent as I grew older where I stood in my stepdad's eyes. One day, I called Mike on his car phone. Yes, my stepdad was probably the only person in Greensboro with a car phone in the early 1990s. Because of his work schedule, I decided to call and ask if he would purchase me a three-subject notebook for school.

"Dad, my English teacher told the class that we need three-subject notebooks. Can you bring one when you come home?"

My request seemed like an urgent request from a child. Nothing crazy. I wasn't asking for a toy, a make-up kit, a prom dress, or a car. I just wanted a notebook for my English class.

"Call your momma and ask her!" he said. "Don't call me asking for a notebook. Your teacher should have told you what you needed before school started. I'm not buying it!" Upset, I hung up the phone.

Later that night, when he came home, my feelings were still hurt. If I were a grown ass man at the time, I probably would have punched him in the face!

"Michael! Come here!" He yelled for my brother to come to the living room. He had a surprise for him.

"Coming, Dad," my brother yelled as he ran down the hallway from his bedroom.

Mike pulled out a black plastic shopping bag and gave it to my brother. My brother's eyes lit up like Christmas morning. He pulled out a box containing a figurine. It was a Crash Dummy Doll that was very popular at the time.

"Oh man! Thanks, Dad!" My brother ran back to his room. My stepdad smiled like he'd just won the father of the year award. I wanted to cry. Just hours earlier, I had asked for a notebook for school and got a third-degree burn, but Mike goes and buys my brother a toy that we all knew would be broken in the next twenty-four hours. Michael-1. Courtney-0.

My brother was a typical teenage boy, but not confrontational. He didn't get into fights. He avoided arguments. He was a good student. Michael was a jokester. He believed everything was funny, and if it wasn't funny, he would try to make it so. He and I had a thing for playing "the boy who cried wolf" games.

"Courtney! There is a fire outside! Come look!"

I got up off my bed with a slight hesitation because I knew how my brother liked to joke around. Walking into the living room and to the front door, I opened the screen door, looking up and down the street for this fire that was supposedly happening.

"Boy, there is nothing outside! Stop messing with me! You get on my nerves!" I yelled with an attitude, walking back to my room.

"Gotcha!" he said, as he laughed this wicked, hard laugh like this was the funniest thing in the world.

"Courtney! The leaves next door are on fire!"

Once again, I sat up and looked at him with annoyance.

"Michael, I'm not messing with you! Go away!"

"No, for real this time! I'm not lying. The leaves are on fire!" he yelled.

For some reason, after the second time he yelled it, there was something different about the tone of his voice. I knew he was serious. I immediately jumped up off my bed and ran to the front door. I could see the haze of smoke billowing in front of our house. I poked my head out of the screen door and looked to the right. Sure enough, the neighbor's pile of leaves that had been raked into a huge pile and never bagged were bursting with flames! By the time I turned around to give my brother direction, he was running out of the kitchen with a cup of water. In my head, I thought he was thirsty, but no, he was going to save the neighborhood from this massive fire with.... his cup of water. Out the door, he ran.

"Michael, hold on!" I yelled, as he ran down the street. I hurried to our outside water hose, hoping it would be long enough to reach the fire or at least long enough that I could arch the water stream to hit the leaves. I ran toward the street, pulling the hose with me, but I suddenly stopped short when the hose reached its limit. Well, here goes nothing. I squeezed the trigger on the handle to arch the water and just as I suspected, the water did NOT reach the fire.

"I'm going to call the fire department!" I told my brother, as he watched in amazement that this was happening.

"Hello, I want to report a fire on Joyce Street. It's a pile of leaves on the side of the street. My brother and I tried to put it out, but we can't." I was so nervous but seemed to handle myself quite well.

Within three minutes, I heard the sirens and horns of what seemed like fifty firetrucks, but it was only three. I believe my brother learned his lesson on this day. Stop lying! What would have happened if I didn't get up? My neighbor's yard and even the house probably would have burned to the ground. Michael never played "gotcha!" again.

During my brother's school years, he was an average student. He was in Boy Scouts for a while and lost interest. He then started playing league baseball and fell in love with it. He was a good player, but eventually, he lost interest in that as well. Dad got him a trumpet to start playing in the school band, and yep, he lost interest in that. He did just enough to pass each grade and graduate from high school. There was some sort of social stigma attached to growing up as a black male—society issued young black boys with unwritten street rules for life that one had to abide by or risk getting bullied, picked on or ostracized because they were not like everyone else.

I think Michael fell into that trap during high school. Again, he was not a bad kid, and we did not grow up in the street life, but because so many of his friends did grow up in the streets or grew up having to figure life out on their own with no guidance, my brother played as if he did as well. I never knew that my mom worried so much about my brother, but I understood why as I got older. My mom and I would regularly talk to my brother about the company he was keeping, the people that he would associate with, and how he could be guilty by association if anything illegal ever happened. In the African-American culture, we were guilty by association more times than not. There was already a stereotypical societal definition of us, i.e., we smoke weed, deal drugs, everyone is on welfare, we are loud and confrontational, we always want to fight, we are disrespectful, we are ignorant, we are lazy, we are thugs, we have deadbeat fathers, all the men are locked up, all the young women are single mothers, etc. If you are with someone who gets caught up in an illegal situation, and you had nothing to do with it, to society, you are guilty and did do it…because you are black.

"Why y'all always got something to say? Dang! I don't need both of y'all jumping down my throat because y'all don't like my friends! They are my friends, not y'all's! You don't have to deal with them. I do."

My brother hated that Mom and I always confronted him with the truth. A hit dog will always bark. The more he got upset, the more I knew that he knew we were right but didn't want to admit to it. Tough love is the hardest love to give, but the most needed love.

"Michael, okay! Keep hanging with the boys down the street and when someone does a drive-by shooting or the police roll up on the house because they are selling weed, don't call Momma or me! We try to protect you, but you don't want to listen!"

I am my brother's keeper. I wanted to wrap my brother in bubble wrap and protect him from the dumb shit happening in the world. I couldn't stand watching him hanging with those thug ass boys, knowing he was not about that life.

"Don't tell him anything, Courtney." My mom was tired and had had enough. "If he gets arrested, I already told him, I'm not bailing him out, and you'd better not either! He wants to be a man, do what he wants to, then he can deal with the consequences that come with his decisions."

It was a rough patch with my brother during his teenage years and into early adulthood, but he was only doing what he knew, what he saw, and what he experienced daily. The environment that surrounded us was raising him. When he would come home at three in the morning without letting Mom know he would be late, or when he would sneak alcohol and fill the liquor bottles up with water, I would ask him, "What were you thinking? Did you think it was okay not coming home until three in the morning and then get upset because Mom was mad at you? Did you truly think that Mom can't taste the water in her mixed drinks?"

I never understood it. My brother had a little arrogance about him due to having been put on a pedestal growing up.

He could do what he wanted and didn't expect consequences to apply to him. He got away with most things, and it carried throughout his years.

There is no doubt that our environments during the early stages of our lives mold us into who we are today. Some of us are strong enough to break that mold, and others are still living in their shell. Luckily, my brother saw the fire before he got burnt, and he understands now why Mom and I stayed on him so hard. A lot of his friends either died at a young age from running the streets or are now locked up. His real friends that are like my little brothers as well, Michael Price and Larry Maynard, have shown him the life of a man. They have been by Michael's side through thick and thin. All three have laughed, cried, and got angry together. Now, they are married with families, and that has slowed my brother down a lot. I thank them for being in my brother's life.

Michael is now a single father, working a management job and living on his own. His eyes are now open to the wisdom my mom and I tried to impart to him. Our relationship is stronger now that we are older. There are still some occasions when my mom calls me complaining about my brother. My response to her is, "Your son is a single father. He is alive. He is not selling drugs. He is not locked up. He doesn't have any warrants. He is not disrespectful. He takes care of his son and has since the day he was born. What is the problem again?" I do this, not to be disrespectful, but to help my mother understand that whatever she is upset about, it could always be worse. Somebody's son is not coming home. A parent somewhere doesn't even know where their son is because the streets kidnapped him. There is a man somewhere not being a father to his child, like myself, and all the child wants is for the dad to come back.

Sometimes, we are not grateful for what we have. We spend some much time dwelling on negative situations in our lives that we forget how to live in the positive. We are greedy with our money, our time, and our love. If we sit back and look at everything around us, what we are complaining about is never that bad.

CHAPTER FOUR

The Strength of a Woman

"**W**hat?! What do you mean Mike has cancer?" Mom exclaimed.

It was a regular Saturday morning. The fall air was crisp. The sun was shining brightly. The leaves on the trees were beginning to turn colors. Aunt Judy had come to visit us from Martinsville, Virginia which was only an hour away. Aunt Judy was my stepdad's sister. Her skin was very light, and she had the blackest, straightest hair down her back. She talked with a country twang that would have you glued to a long conversation just to hear her speak. Aunt Judy was the fun aunt. She once took Michael and me to the movies to see Teenage Mutant Ninja Turtles on opening day! For young kids, how cool was that! My stepdad and his sister were very close.

That morning in the kitchen, Mom and aunt Judy were cleaning up and washing dishes when Aunt Judy dropped the bombshell on my mother.

"You mean Mike ain't tell you? Yeah, he called me the other day and said he finally went to the doctor to run some tests because he was feeling funny. He thought he had sclerosis of the liver, but they told him it was cancer. Gwen, you gotta talk to him and see what is going on."

My stepdad hated going to the doctor. No matter how much my mom would ask about him getting a check-up, he flat-out refused. Mom was no-nonsense. She believed in taking care of yourself. Every six months, my brother and I were at the dentist's office like clockwork. We got physicals every year. If anything hurt on our bodies, to the doctor's office we went!

I was fourteen when we finally found out Mike had colon cancer. At that time, cancer was not talked about or on the forefront of every television commercial as it is now. It was November 1995. At first, nothing changed except for his eating habits. I noticed he no longer ate the things he liked before like fried fish, chicken, and potatoes. He complained about how everything he ate and drank felt so thick in his mouth, and he would get full very quickly. Mom became the breadwinner in the house once Mike was unable to work. I would walk by my stepdad resting on the living room couch with his legs propped up, looking frail and weak. His feet and legs were so swollen that the skin on his legs and feet were tight and shiny. It was extremely hurtful for me to see the man of our house in this vulnerable state, and there was nothing I could do take away his pain. I didn't know how to communicate with him. I didn't know what to say, so I would brush past him as if he wasn't there. The decision was made to place Mike on in-home hospice care. Soon after, his baby brother, Uncle Robert, moved in with us to help take care of his brother.

Monday, April 15, 1996, it was six in the morning when I woke up to get ready for school. My stepfather could no longer take care of himself. Mom was doing her now usual routine of bathing him in bed, changing his diaper, and cleaning his bedpan. Uncle Robert was moving about the house, and my brother was up as well. As I was combing my hair in the mirror of my dresser, I began to hear loud moans. It sounded like a tribal leader was humming the sound of his people. It was a deep baritone, and something in my stomach told me that this was not good.

Mike was dying…in the house, at that very moment. I walked out of my room and looked across the hall. There he was in bed. His eyes were wide open, gray, and glossed over. His head was tilted back, and his mouth was open. He looked as though he was asking God to take him now. In my heart, I knew he was ready. With this being too much for me, I quickly walked down the hall, prepared to go to my bus stop, eager to get out of the house. My brother, sensing something was wrong, asked Mom if he could stay home. She agreed. Michael sat in the bedroom, in his dad's wheelchair, fixated on what was happening. Waiting at the bus stop, I saw the bus looming larger as it made its way toward my stop. Something came over me like a chill, but I wasn't cold. I just froze. It was like the earth got quiet, and time stopped. When the bus stopped, I snapped out of my daze, got myself together, and boarded. Quietly, I rode the bus to school, thinking about the moans and seeing Mike's eyes wide open. It was a movie stuck on replay in my head. I went directly to my NJROTC class once I arrived at school. I wanted so badly to get somewhere where something would take my mind off what was happening at my house.

My anxiety was extremely high as I sat at my desk, thinking about my mom and my brother who I left behind. My chest was tight, and my hands were clammy. I didn't want to talk to anyone. I tried to black out, wake up, and see that this was all a bad dream. Then an announcement came through the classroom speaker.

"SGT Jarrell, is Courtney Kittrell in your class? I need her to report to the admin office." At that very moment, I knew Mike was dead. As I slowly opened the door to the school's administration office, my Grandma Ann turned around. Her nose and cheeks were red. Her bottom lip started quivering.

"Baby, I'm so sorry," she said.

I collapsed in the middle of the office. No matter how much we think we are ready for death, we are never ready. We prepare ourselves through our thoughts on how life will be when the time comes, but we are never truly ready for anyone to die. Grandma took me to the hospital to meet up with my family.

At the hospital, I kept a close watch on my mom. I could not imagine the pain she was feeling at that time. The man who rescued her and her daughter, the man who supported our family and gave unconditional love the only way he knew how was now dead. But like a strong black woman, she held herself together with poise, confidence, and grace. She took charge, making decisions and phone calls as if this was just business. Any other person would think she was acting coldhearted, but that was not the case. A situation like the one she was facing tests your mind, your adrenaline, and your strength. Sometimes, we deflect the truth even though its right in front of us because we are scared and unsure of what is going to happen next. So, we stay busy, conducting, organizing, moving about, and multi-tasking until we are ready to face reality.

My Aunt Rosemary took me to the viewing room. I walked in slowly. Mike was dressed in a white hospital gown, lying on his back on the table, draped with a white crisp hospital sheet up to chest level. His once-frail body had tripled in size because it was swollen with fluid buildup. I broke down. My tears flowed by the gallons. Despite everything, Mike kept me for twelve years. Despite everything, he provided for my mother, brother, and me. Despite everything, he was human. He was someone's son, brother, uncle, nephew, father, and grandfather. He was somebody. Sure, he wasn't perfect. Mom and Mike once had a domestic battery case when Mike thought Mom was cheating on him, but she wasn't. He fought with her outside the house at two o'clock in the morning in front of my brother and me, but still, my mother loved him. He didn't take my mom on dates or bring her flowers just because, or get her fancy expensive jewelry on Christmas, but still my mother upheld "...till death do us part..." Mike had flaws, but we all do! I cried because I never told him thank you! I cried because that one time I saw him slumped over on the bed with no strength to sit up, I helped him without speaking a word to him. I missed that opportunity to say, "I love you." To ask him how he was feeling, to have a five-minute conversation. I cried because I had been selfish and didn't realize the value in him until he was gone.

There was little life insurance, and our lives changed dramatically. K-Mart went bankrupt, and my mom lost her job after twenty-three years. Seeing her at a brick wall was not real to me. This woman was the foundation of my being. She took care of her dying husband, even after he laid hands on her. She upheld her wedding vows. Now, she was scrambling trying to figure out the next steps in life. Where to go. What job to get. The next paycheck. She had lost her husband. Now, she was losing her job.

A couple of years later, my maternal grandmother was diagnosed with multiple myeloma cancer. Sickness could not be happening again. Not to the queen of our family! My mother was there for her mom, making trips to Fayetteville every chance she got. Even though my mother was not the only child, sometimes it felt like she was the only one who cared. My aunt Nancy lived in Atlanta, Georgia with her husband and two sons. My aunt Ruthie resided in Columbia, South Carolina with her husband and four children. My uncle Rudy, well, no one knew where he was because drugs snatched him away from the family. With two capable and able sisters, my mother was the only one who constantly ensured my grandmother was getting her medical care. My grandfather relied on Mom's strength as well to help out around the house and with my grandmother.

"Gwen, I'm calling the ambulance to come to get your mother. She is not waking up."

"Daddy, what do you mean she is not waking up? Is she breathing?"

"Yes, she is breathing. I don't know, darling. We will see what the doctors say when we get to the hospital. Can you come down here?"

"Yeah. I'm coming as soon as I get myself together."

In November 2006 my grandmother went into a deep sleep, almost coma-like. As always, mom was by her father's side. Granddad was tired. He was on the verge of losing his life partner of fifty years.

"Courtney, I'm at the hospital with Granddad. Momma won't wake up, and the doctors are running tests now to see what is going on."

"What? Are you serious? How is Granddaddy holding up? Is he okay?" I couldn't believe this phone call. In my head, I thought this can't be life. I just lost my stepdad not too long ago, and now my grandmother? In September, my grandparents spent their anniversary with me in Virginia Beach, Virginia. I wasn't all too excited about the visitation, but there is a reason for everything. My grandmother wanted to attend a taping of the Christian program, 700 Club, which is filmed at Regent University in Virginia Beach. It's definitely not a young adult's dream, but it was what my grandmother wanted so I complied. I took my grandmother to the beach for the first time in her life, to Naval Station Oceana's Master Jet Base to watch fighter jets take off and land, and then a yacht lunch date onboard the Spirit of Norfolk, where I observed, for the first time in my life, my grandparents dancing together on the dance floor. Two months later, she was unresponsive, and we didn't know if she was going to live or die.

December 2006, I received word that my grandmother died in the hospital. My world fell apart. Not for me, but my mother. She had buried her husband, and now she had to bury her mother. Granddad had spent fifty years with a woman who took care of the home while he was off fighting in Vietnam. Fifty years with the woman who raised four kids to the best of her ability with no complaints. Fifty years of marriage, through thick and thin, for better or worse. Now, she had been called home because she completed the will of God. It hurt me to see my mother and my grandfather lose their first loves. In addition to all that was going on with my grandmother, we would soon come to learn my Aunt Nancy was battling a crisis herself.

Aunt Nancy was my mother's oldest sister. My mom looked up to her big sister and her success. She worked for Proctor and Gamble for a while but soon became heavily involved in Avon. Aunt Nancy married her college sweetheart, Darrell Turner, and they had two sons, Robert and James. Uncle Darrell's job in the computer field moved the family from Atlanta, GA overseas to the Netherlands for a couple of years. While there, my uncle noticed that Nancy was starting to forget simple things. She would go to put gas in the car and couldn't remember how to get home. He once came home, and she was wearing layers upon layers of clothing. Aunt Nancy would cook food and forget it was on the stove or in the oven, almost burning down the house. Uncle Darrell began taking her to doctors, but they couldn't give a clear reason as to why my aunt was so forgetful. So, he did what he had to do for his wife, and the family moved back to Atlanta. Things started to become noticeable after my grandmother's death.

"Aye y'all, while the men are shopping for suit jackets for Mom's funeral, let's go to Ross Department store and see if we can find something for them," said Aunt Nancy. My mom, Aunt Nancy, Aunt Ruthie and I were together in Nancy's car. My brother and Uncle Darrell wanted to find nice suit jackets to wear to the funeral, so we went out shopping. We parked in the lot of the shopping center. I was in the back seat with Aunt Ruthie. Mom was in the front passenger seat, and aunt Nancy in the driver's seat.

"Yeah. Let's do that!" Mom said.

"OK. Let me call Darrell to let him know where we are going."

Aunt Nancy pulled out her cellphone, and for a good ten solid minutes, she scrolled and scrolled through her phone. At the time, I didn't know what was happening. My mother picked up on it and said," Nancy, did you forget what you were doing?"

"Huh? What do you mean?"

I could tell from the confused look on my aunt's face that she did indeed forget what she was doing. We never made it to Ross Department Store, and my mother never brought it up. We left and drove back to my grandparents' house.

Over time, my mom stayed engaged with my uncle about my aunt's health. She was diagnosed with dementia and was rapidly deteriorating before our eyes. Also, with my aunt's illness, her oldest son, my cousin Robert, enlisted in the National Guard, was attacked by an IED while deployed in Afghanistan. He was diagnosed with PTSD and was living at home. My uncle was struggling with dealing with the blows of life. Aunt Nancy, by this time, stopped communicating and walking entirely, and my cousin who never slept believed "they" were coming to kill him, so he started collecting guns and could not keep a job. Mom drove to Atlanta whenever she could to help take care of her oldest sister without a second thought. I was so nervous for my family. Collecting guns was not a thing that my cousin was previously into. I would worry about Robert being so paranoid and not being able to handle his PTSD, that he would ultimately kill his parents in a fit of rage.

May 27, 2015, my feisty, stylish, undeniably intelligent, strong independent aunt lost her life. Forty-four years of marriage to my uncle and fifty-seven years of being a big sister to my mother. Mom made it through, yet again, without missing a beat. I don't think I ever saw my mom cry.

We take our mothers for granted. They carry life's heaviest loads usually without a "Thank you." Without a thought, women are the ones who raise and maintain the family. They are the ones who are depended upon to guide a child through his or her life. Women are raised from the womb to find the men of their dreams, settle down, get married, have children, build a career, and live happily ever after. When we are upset, we want the embrace of our mother. When we need tough love, we look for our mothers, and when we need a calming touch, we look for our mothers. One day, Mother will not be around. Her will on earth will be done, and she will be called home. Don't miss the opportunity to love and appreciate your mom while she is above ground. One day, it might be too late.

I cherish my mother. She is strong with her love, her compassion, her commitment, her dedication, her empathy, her unselfishness, and devotion to those around her, not just her family. She has been the rock of our family and continues to make a difference every day and carry the load for my grandfather, my brother, and myself. Her strength is undeniable.

CHAPTER FIVE

Finding My Crown

Growing up, my mother taught me to be independent. I learned how to be a strong woman by watching her. Her influence was huge. I didn't know life's purpose or who I was supposed to be. I went with the normal flow of school, boyfriends, and part-time jobs. I wasn't a very social kid. I had friends but no cliques. I wasn't among the popular girls. I had no confidence in myself. I was quiet, just trying to figure out this thing called life and my purpose.

I had a cousin, Jeanine, who was the best cousin a kid could have. She was much older than my brother and me. In the fourth grade, my brother and I became latchkey kids, meaning we came home from school by ourselves until our parents came home from work. Jeanine would usually meet us at the bus stop and walk us home. She was light-skinned, tall, skinny, had straight black hair that she kept cut short on top with a long rat tail in the back. She had tattoos on her arms that looked like they were done in a prison cell, a missing front tooth, and always had a Budweiser beer can in her hand. She hung with shady-looking guys who were known as her "boyfriends," but they weren't. She looked just like a boy and walked like a boy. Jeanine had boyish mannerisms, but in my eyes, Jeanine was cool! Who would mess with her? She looked tough. I loved her so much but didn't know why I wanted to be close to her all the time. It was something about her that connected me to her and made me feel comfortable.

It is very unfortunate that America has a mold in which everyone is to fit. Men and women are to marry only. Women are to support the husband. The husband is to work and provide for the family—two children per household. Anything outside this, and society shuns you. How dare you go against the perfect family and biblical ways. I had boyfriends during my high school years, same as so-called normal girls. I had the picture-perfect wedding ideas with the two children, one boy, and one girl. I didn't know anything else. My environment was raising me. What I did know was that even though I had boyfriends, I wasn't sexually attracted to them. Yeah, I know…sexually attracted to boys in high school? It is a real thing. High school years are when your hormones start to mature. You are old enough to know what males and females are supposed to do besides hold hands. You hear stories of other couples and even meet some teenagers who are now parents because there was no push for sex education, and you are left to explore sex for yourself. I explored sex at the age of sixteen and became pregnant. The first time was all it took.

"Oh my God, Courtney! I can't believe you! You are a child! I can't do this...I can't do this." My mother was so disappointed in me. I knew I had let her down. It felt like there was 1,000 pounds of pressure on me and time was standing still. The trouble was not getting any lighter. I didn't know what to say.

"I know, Mom. I'm so sorry! I didn't mean for this to happen. I swear I didn't!"

"You are not keeping it. I don't want you to ruin your life and struggle going through high school with a baby! Are you freaking kidding me? Who is the father?" My mom wanted to talk to the young man and his mother.

"His name is Lionel. We go to school together. He is a junior."

Lionel was a charming guy. He was light-skinned, athletic and funny. He had a very young, boyish look and the biggest smile I had ever seen. I liked him because he wasn't popular, but everyone knew him. He was a very humble young man and knew the value of family. Lionel didn't have the best life growing up. He lived in a small apartment with his mother and baby sister. He had five siblings, and they were very close. Lionel didn't have a lot, but he lived his best life. Nothing got in his way. He never had a bad day. Because he excelled in his academics, I knew Lionel was going to have a bright future.

"We're going to his house right now! Get your shit and let's go!"

We started driving to Lionel's house, which was only about eight minutes from my house. In the car, I could see the pain on my mother's face. I could see her asking what she did wrong with me. She didn't do anything wrong. Society did it. Wanting to see what it was like, what all the hype was about is what did it. Hell, I didn't even have an orgasm. So, I still had not "experienced" sex. I wasn't even turned on. Not because I didn't like Lionel, but because I would find out in a couple of years that everything that was meant for everybody else was not meant for me.

I had an abortion at sixteen. An abortion! Going into the doctor's office, I felt so ashamed. How did I let it come to this? I knew better. The procedure is something no woman ever forgets. Your body is disrespected and violated. The operation is so routine that no one cares about how you are feeling afterward. No one knows the emotional scar you will wear the rest of your life or the pain of thinking about the "what ifs." When it was over, I wanted to curl up in a bathtub and cry. I killed my baby. I took a life. The struggle of morals and ethics is real. It took me a while to adjust to that. I know things are done and happen for a reason, but in reality, I did this to myself. Years went by, and I would wonder what my baby would have looked like. Would he or she have my dimples, Lionel's nose, or my long eyelashes? Would they be smart and ambitious? I dreamt about how I would have raised my child— reading to them every night, doing homework, going to museums, etc. I had my entire life planned out in my head, what it would have been like, but life is not always perfect. There are plans for our lives that we don't know.

After Lionel and I broke up, I continued to date guys. I had sex, but still nothing: no excitement, no orgasm. I bounced from boy to boy, thinking these little boys couldn't handle me and that is why they didn't turn me on. The real problem was not the males. It was me. I was not sexually attracted to men. I didn't have a problem telling a guy I thought he was cute or fine or had a beautiful body, but that was as far as it would go. I knew it but didn't want to face it.

I remember at seven years old staying at my great Aunt Future's house as she babysat my brother and me. Her son, my cousin Wayne, was a lot older than I and had Playboy magazines. The magazines were stacked on the end table in the living room next to my aunt's Good Housekeeping magazines. I'd sneak the Playboy magazine inside the Good Housekeeping magazine, so no one knew what I was really looking at. The assumption would be that I was interested in gardening and home floor plans. I knew then, as a seven-year-old, that girls looking at girls was "wrong," so that was why I hid the Playboy magazine. I was so fixated on the female anatomy in all of its beauty. I was mesmerized but did not understand what that meant.

So now, being older, I was at the crossroads of trying to find myself and who I was meant to be. I couldn't and wouldn't say, "I'm gay." Acknowledgement takes a lot of strength. Coming out of the closet takes courage for those who are gay. People have a natural fear of the unknown. They will use their fight or flight instincts to deal with a situation that scares them. They can either fight for what they believe in and to be heard or they can run and hide and stay hidden in their personal closet or prison—running away from who they are. For a gay person, opening up to family and friends is very stressful. They don't know if their family will be accepting of them or disown them because they don't understand, so it is easier to push away.

A lot of the time we feel as though we are letting our parents down because we know they want the best for us. Parents want their children to succeed and do better than they did. Having a child who is gay can make a parent feel as though, they didn't do enough or raise their child correctly. They truth is everything isn't for everybody. One size definitely DOES NOT fit all! I once had a conversation with my mother and she told me I hadn't met the right guy. I asked my mom if she liked coconut. I knew she didn't, and she answered no. I told her she just hadn't found the right one yet. That conversation was never held again.

The only person I knew who could have been gay was my cousin Jeanine, but by this time, she had died. It was just me in a world with no direction, no clarification, mentorship, nothing. I was on my own. I had my best friend Shameka at the time, but still, telling her that I thought I liked girls was not an option. Then, I would lose the one friend I had. I already had to deal with getting pregnant and seeing the look of shame on my mother's face—the one person a child never wants to disappoint. I mean, my family went to church. I was an usher, Mom was an usher, and Dad and Pastor were close friends. I sang in the choir and attended bible study every Wednesday night. Having to listen to people talk about going to hell, living in sin, and feeling like I would be a disappointment kept me from talking to anybody about what I was going through internally. I was stressed out at an early age. I did not have confidence to stand up and speak for myself. I didn't have enough life experience and strength to not give in to ignorant remarks about homosexuals. Having these feelings can leave a person feeling like a prisoner in their own world. They feel abandoned, alone, worthless, hopeless, and depressed. Some of us are lucky in that we have supportive families and friends. Some don't have anybody, and they turn to the streets and drugs to take away or fill the void in their lives. All because they have no one to talk to.

Maybe if I ignore the way I feel, it will go away! That is what I thought and what I did. I ignored my feelings and suppressed them by dating guys. I played to America's societal rules; living the normal life and toeing the line. I would go on to keep my secret until my early twenties. I went as far as getting married to a guy because I was drunk on New Year's Eve when he popped the question, and I said, "Yes." That marriage would be the pivotal point in my life where I would find the strength to step out of my closet and my personal prison. Through pain, heartache, failures, and lost love, I would begin the process of walking in my purpose and finally finding my crown.

CHAPTER SIX

D. E. P.

As my time in high school was coming to an end, I wasn't sure of what I wanted to do with my life. I knew I did not want to stay in Greensboro forever. I wanted to explore outside the city. See what else was in the world. I knew mom did not have money for college. I never applied for any scholarships. I did, however, take an A.S.V.A.B. test and passed when I was NJROTC just in case I wanted to join the military. I loved the discipline, military bearing, and professionalism that a person in a uniform exuded. At a young age, Granddaddy taught me how to polish shoes, Grandma taught me how to do 45-degree angles with the bed sheets, and I was ready!

I would watch as young soldiers from the Army would set up their display table in the cafeteria, trying to entice young lost souls to be a part of something greater than them. I took the bait. For three long months, Sgt. Pool called my phone and sold everything but the stars to me, trying to enlist me in the Army. Divine intervention happened, and for some reason, I stopped answering and responding to his requests, even though I loved the benefits of what he would tell me. I wanted it all, but not with the Army, not in the woods with a tent, not stationed in Germany for forever. I made the decision that I wanted to join the Navy, but I had to cross over the parental lines.

"Mr. Kittrell, I promise Courtney is going to be taken care of. All we need is your signature saying you are okay with us taking her to MEPS for her medical screening. She is not being shipped off to boot camp. We are just making sure she is qualified if she wants to join the Navy." Petty Officer Byrd, my Navy recruiter, was draining low on patience.

"Dad, sign the papers! I'm coming back! I'm just going to Charlotte to do my medical screening." By this time, I was over it. It felt like eight hours had passed by, and my dad was stubborn as hell, not wanting me to go anywhere. I was finishing my senior year in high school, so I was not going anywhere anytime soon. My biological dad recently moved back to Greensboro during this time, and I guess he was trying to play catch up with my life, so now he was acting like a father.

"Mr. Kittrell, I know you want the best for your daughter. We are going to give her the best. You have to trust us. Your signature is all we need." My recruiter was doing his best to persuade my dad. My dad looked at me with sadness in his eyes. "Is this what you want, baby girl?"

"Yes, daddy!" I said, but what I wanted to say was, "Nigga sign these muthafucking papers right the fuck now!

It took you seventeen years to come back in my life and now you want to be a daddy? Nigga, please! You are about to see what it feels like when someone walks away from you!"

I enlisted in the Delayed Entry Program for the Navy. Once I passed my medical screening in November of 1998, I was slated to go to boot camp the following year after I graduated from high school. This idea was terrific to me. I was excited about doing something different with my life. I watched as girls in high school become young, black, single, teenage mothers, and I knew that was not what I wanted. I had a purpose for my life and just didn't know it. I had the opportunity to do better. I had the chance to show that world that there are women who are strong, independent, and willing to make a difference in the world, to be a role model. I was still sad about my pregnancy though, but would I even have had the opportunity to join the Navy if I became a young, black, single, teenage mother? Things happen for a reason. We never know what that reason is until we look back at things in retrospect.

I graduated from James B. Dudley High School in May 1999 and left for Recruit Training Command in Great Lakes, Il July 30, 1999. I was eighteen years old.

"I'm going to miss you so much!" My mother squeezed me as we stood in the parking lot of the recruiting office. All the prospect recruits and their families huddled around, saying their goodbyes as their babies were headed off to begin new lives.

"Oh, Momma, you will be okay! You told me I had to leave the house when I turned eighteen. Look at me now! I am grown and gone!"

We laughed, but I knew she was scared for me. Her oldest child, who was her sounding board and her rib, was leaving for an indefinite period.

"Okay, niece! You listen to what the Recruit Division Commanders tell you! Keep your mouth shut. Ain't this something?" My Uncle Tim had been my number one fan and the third father in my life. He has always been there through my entire career, asking questions and catching up on how the Navy has changed since his retirement. Talking with him gets me excited because he instills his passion for success in me and makes me feel proud of every career move I make. I am truly thankful for him, his wisdom and experience that he has passed down to me since the day he found out I wanted to join the Navy.

Uncle Tim retired as a Petty Officer First Class Postal Clerk from the Navy after dealing with a traumatic event that almost cost him his life. To this day, he is still recovering and dealing with the emotional side of it. Post-traumatic stress disorder is real, and it is more common than people know. During my recruitment, I used Uncle Tim as my sounding board. He made sure the recruiters were not feeding my mom and I bullshit. In the beginning, I wanted to be a Hospital Corpsman, but the Navy said no because there were too many females in that job field. My recruiter was giving me a list of jobs that I qualified for based on my ASVAB score. I made a 50. It wasn't too bad, so I had a couple of jobs I could select.

"We can put you in for Ship's Storekeeper."

"What do they do?" I asked. "I'm not trying to do anything stupid! Don't be slick!"

I had heard about recruiters giving applicants information to make a decision seem reasonable, but in the end, it would be the worst decision ever! He was not going to try me this day!

"Let me think about it and get back to you." I told him. I had a plan and I was not going to be pressured into some bullshit, especially when it was my life. I spoke to my uncle and my mother about it.

"Uncle Tim, what is a Ship's Storekeeper?" Uncle Tim's duty stations were primarily ships, so I knew he had the answers to my questions.

"Is that what the recruiter offered you?" he asked.

"Yeah. Petty Officer Byrd said I would be working on the ships, but the job ain't that bad. He said something about me stocking vending machines, doing laundry, and cutting hair. Y'all got a barbershop on a ship?"

I did not know anything about the Navy. I was shocked to hear of a ship having a barbershop. What if the boat rocked side to side while you were getting your hair cut? I had so many questions!

"No! You are not going to be anybody's storekeeper! You planning on running your own store or a dry-cleaning business or working for Pepsi when you get out?" he asked.

"Hell no!" I said.

That was not for me or my future. I was a girly girl. I could not see myself doing any of those things.

"I'm taking you back to the recruiter and talking to them myself. They tried it." Uncle Tim was serious, and I was so grateful.

With advice from my uncle, mom and I went to the recruiting station the next day, and she gave the recruiters a piece of her mind.

"Courtney told me you are trying to put her in the Navy as an SH. I don't want her cutting hair and stocking vending machines for the rest of her life. Y'all gotta do better than this, or she is not going."

A piece of me wanted to die from embarrassment, and another part of me was the hype man behind my mom, screaming, "Hell yeah! I ain't going no damn where unless you change my shit!"

My recruiter pulled out a secret book that contained information on Aviation Ratings. It was like mom hit the jack pot!

"Don't tell anyone I am showing this book to you." he said.

Mom flipped through the book showing me endless pages of job options. I was overwhelmed. I knew that whatever I chose, I wanted to be successful and have something to carry over if and when I decided I did not want to continue in the Navy.

"Okay. Well, I can put Courtney in as an Undesignated Airman." my recruiter said.

"What is that?" I asked.

"You go into the aviation field. You won't have a specific job, but once you get to your first duty station, you can choose whatever job you want."

"Okay. That sounds a little bit better. At least, I will have an option."

"Is this what you want?" mom asked. "I think this is better for you. What do you think?"

"I'll take it!" And just like that, I was on a new course with a new direction in life.

In the parking lot, the recruiters told us to hurry with our goodbyes so we could get on the road. Little did I know where this road would take me, how many bumps would be on this road, how many times I would want to drive off the road, how many passengers I would bring down the road with me, and how many passengers I would leave behind. This road would start my journey, and it would be the hardest road I would endure. My strength, my motivation, my comeback, my voice, and my life would all be paved by this road. It was my time to get in the van.

CHAPTER SEVEN

Navy

J uly 30, 1999 was a warm and humid night. The sky was patchy with clouds. The moon was shining brightly. I arrived at Recruit Training Command Great Lakes, Il on a bus with forty-nine other recruits, anxious and scared as hell. Eager to get boot camp over with and terrified of what the next eight weeks were going to entail. The doors to the bus opened, and all hell broke loose!

"GET OFF THE BUS! MOVE! MOVE! MOVE!"

I scrambled, trying to gather all my belongings as all of us recruits were hurriedly escorted off the bus and into building 1405 also known as the Golden Thirteen in honor of the first thirteen African-American Commissioned Naval Officers.

"As you go into the building, you will place your envelope in the basket provided on the table! Do you understand? Once you get inside the building, you better not step on my flags! All the females line up on the right side of the flags, and all the males form up on the left side of the flags. Side by side! You are facing each other!" Petty Officer was giving us so many instructions at once. I felt so overwhelmed! My main focus at this moment was trying to remember everything we were instructed to do so I would not get into trouble on my very first night. Shit just got real!

I had spent the day before I left for boot camp at home, doing absolutely nothing. I was nervous and thinking about not going through with it at all. I decided to watch G. I. Jane, a movie with Demi Moore about how she was tortured, picked on, degraded, and shamed by all the alpha males. They believed women were weak and not meant to be in the military. I was in a state of panic and fright my first night.

"Your momma and daddy are not here to save you! You all are grown adults and will be treated as such. You will only speak when spoken to. When you do speak, you will say Aye, Aye Petty Officer, Chief, Senior Chief, Master Chief, etc. Do you understand?"

All the recruits shouted, "Yes, Petty Officer!"

We were all lined up accordingly, and the Company Commanders were going through paperwork and gathering necessary items.

"As I call your name, say your entire social security number out loud to me so I can verify who you are. There is no 'O' in the numerical system, only 'zero'. 'O' is not a number! Do you understand?"

"Aye, Aye, Petty Officer!" we all shouted.

Oh boy. So much information to process. In my head, I practiced saying zero versus O. I kept telling myself I got it. Just say zero, and everything will be okay. Besides, this was my first instruction, I'd better not mess this up. When it was my turn, wouldn't you know it? I shouted "O" at the top of my lungs. My world stopped. Petty Officer stopped, and it was over. As Petty Officer walked closer toward me, I heard his footsteps get louder and louder. I wanted to die right there on the spot. Yep…mom was not here to save me. Jesus, where are you?!

"Recruit! Didn't I tell you there is no 'O' in the numerical system? Are you sure you can handle instructions?" Petty Officer was a half-millimeter from my face. His breath was hot, and his face was not pleasant. This was not how it was supposed to go. I mean I just practiced everything in my head. Damn! As the Petty Officer was yelling at me, I did the nervous smile thing, unbeknownst to myself. That wasn't a thing I knew I did. My smile quickly set him off.

"Are you freaking smiling at me now?! Do you think this is a game? Wipe that damn smile off your face, recruit! I can tell it is going to be a long eight weeks for you!"

He grew to be seven feet tall and was towering over me. Oh, lord! Just get me out of this mess. I wanted to go home and say Fuck it! I tried!

"Turn around and face the bulkhead until you wipe the shit-eating grin off your face and get your crap together!"

"Aye, Aye, Petty Officer!" I yelled.

I executed that order with smooth quickness! Petty Officer-1. Seaman Recruit Kittrell-0. Welcome to boot camp.

Every Sailor's boot camp experience is different. I tried to stay low-key and do as I was told. Because of my NJROTC experience, I was in a 900 division, which is a performing division. Recruits who are part of a 900 division participate in the choir, rifle team, state flags and drum line, and perform for every graduation ceremony. Our boot camp routine was slightly different from the rest of the divisions because the recruits had to practice with their respective performance areas.

My division was an integrated division. We had male and female recruits. We were the state flags division, and I was a part of the choir. We sang for graduations and were invited to perform at local community events. On one occasion, we were asked to sing the National Anthem for Flag Day at North Chicago High School, about two miles from RTC. About eight females from my division would be a part of this event. Our Company Commander, Petty Officer Swain, instructed us not to eat or drink anything but water.

"Your shipmates cannot have any candy or soda, so you better not eat or drink anything but water!" Petty Officer shouted. Petty Officer Swain was a short, stout, white female. Her hair was dirty blond, cut short, and her bangs in front were always feathered to the left side. Her skin was tan, and I could tell that under her short-sleeve summer white uniform top, she had a farmer's tan. A very aggressive female, she had a harsh, stern voice, and she never smiled.

Petty Officer walked aggressively like a guy and owned an entire room when she entered. Even though she was short, her attitude and demeanor made her out to be at least six feet tall. It was a privilege for us to be allowed off base during boot camp. The Navy has a motto, "One Team, One Fight." Whatever your team is doing, is what you are to do. Since our shipmates back at boot camp could not eat or drink anything sweet and tempting, we were forbidden to eat or drink the same at our event.

"This is one team, one fight! If your shipmates can't have it, you can't either! Do you understand?!"

"Aye, Aye, Petty Officer!" all the girls shouted.

As we rode the activity bus to the high school, one of the female recruits was put in charge of the rest of us. I saw the stress on her face having to babysit seven grown females and scared of us doing something stupid to get her in trouble. This was going to be her first taste of leadership.

"When we get off the bus, don't eat or drink anything. Okay. I don't want to get in trouble." She was terrified, and her voice was cracking. This was about to be interesting.

I leaned into her and said, "Who is going to know if we eat or drink anything if we don't say nothing? I say we do what we want, and if you get in trouble, I will go down with you."

I meant every word I told her. You see, my thought process was that if we did enjoy ourselves and have a piece of candy or a sip of soda, how would Petty Officer find out if we didn't say anything. One team, one fight, right?

"Stop being so damn scared! I'm going to have fun!" I told her. We were free from boot camp for almost a day. I was going to enjoy my freedom before I returned to hell!

The bus parked. Our choir director was a Senior Chief. His exact words to us, before we departed the bus, were "Y'all have fun! Eat and be merry! "Now, I don't know if he was serious or joking, but what I do know is that I was taught in boot camp to follow the last direct order. That is precisely what I did.

The choir sang the National Anthem and we received a standing ovation. I was proud. I was a part of something bigger than myself for the first time and I was elated. We were dismissed to enjoy the activities around us. The event was set up like a county fair on a high school football field. There were food vendors, small amusement rides, and people everywhere. I found a food stand that sold candy. All I could think of was plain M&Ms. My favorite candy. The lady at the stand gave me a free bag, and I was in heaven. I walked around, taking in all the sights and looking at the smiles on the kids' faces. I could not wait to graduate and live my life.

On the bus ride back to boot camp, some of us were trying to take a quick nap. The young lady in charge of us was sweating the fact that some of us enjoyed our outing a little too much.

"We are in so much trouble! Petty Officer is going to find out y'all had candy, and we are going to get beat!" she said out loud.

"Girl, shut up! The only people who know are us. I know I'm not going to tell on myself. The only way Petty Officer will know is if your dumbass says something. Stop being stupid! But, if she does find out and you get in trouble, I will go down with you as I promised."

I could not believe this girl would be so stupid to tell on us. I knew then, at that moment, that people are cut from a different cloth. I was raised not to be a snitch. You don't tell on yourself and get yourself in trouble. That is plain dumb, but yet here we are. I was never afraid of getting in trouble for eating candy. I was fearful of this scary ass female running her mouth because she did not have street sense.

We arrived back at boot camp around 1700. Our division was eating dinner. We were instructed to change out of our dress uniforms into our utility uniforms and catch up with the rest of our division at chow. As we were changing our clothes, some of the girls were pulling bags of Skittles out of their socks and putting them away in their locked drawers. I was bold but not that bold. We giggled quietly because we knew what was up. If you had contraband, you were going to give it up, get beaten, or take a chance of someone telling on you because you didn't share with them.

"Aye, get in the freaking office right now!" Petty Officer Swain came out of nowhere, yelling.

We scrambled into her office half-dressed in our uniforms.

"I want to know who the idiot was that talked to Senior Chief about y'all eating candy! Didn't I give specific instructions that you were not to eat or drink anything but water? You thought this was a joke?" she shouted.

We were lined up in the office in two rows of four. I was standing in the front row, staring out of the big glass window that faced into our compartment. You could see everything; all the racks, the tables, the end of the compartment and the coat hooks that held our raincoats.

"What part of one team, one fight, don't you understand? So, who the hell talked to Senior Chief?" she asked. Her face was red. I felt terrible but not that bad. I wanted to fight whoever said anything about our outing. It was quiet. None of the females wanted to answer. We knew what our fate was about to be. We were going to make it rain in the compartment.

Making it rain meant that the RDC was going to exercise us with no ending in sight. With the sweat from our bodies, the compartment would start to get humid, and moisture build-up would happen along the walls and ceiling. Soon, drops of water would begin falling.

"It was me, Petty Officer. I did it," said the scary ass female.

I was so pissed! This broad talked to Senior Chief about us eating candy? Now all of us were getting in trouble!

"Line up in front of your racks now!" Petty Officer yelled.

All of us ran to the front of our racks. I knew what was going to happen next.

"Jumping jacks! Begin!" Swain yelled.

"One, two, three…ONE! One, two, three… TWO…"

As we were having our deficiencies corrected, I looked over at that female. She was crying. I wanted to yell to her, "Shut that shit up! It is your fault. You did this. You snitched, and now you're crying because these arm circles hurt! You should have had M&Ms with the rest of us, so at least it would have been worth it for you." That experience taught me not to trust anyone automatically. You have to earn that.

CHAPTER EIGHT

Schooled in More Ways than One

graduated Recruit Training Command in October 1999. My mom and dad attended my graduation ceremony. I received my first set of orders to VAW-121, a squadron, onboard Naval Air Station Oceana in Norfolk, VA. Before I was due to check in at my new command, I was to attend Airman Apprenticeship Training also known as ATD school in Pensacola, Florida. The school was to familiarize me with aviation jobs, terminology and aircraft. It provided the fundamentals I would need to get started in my new career.

My class instructor was a First-Class Petty Officer, which is the rank of an E-6. He was African American, wore glasses, and had an overgrown fade that was overdue for a haircut. He had a no-shave chit because his face and neck would bump up if he did shave. His beard was scruffy and unkempt. His fingers looked like little sausages, and he was very overweight. His short-sleeve, light blue, utility uniform shirt looked like it stretched beyond limits because his stomach hung over his pants. I was amazed. After all the beatings and workouts I endured in boot camp, I left thinking the Navy was all about enforcing fitness and healthy lifestyle habits. My instructor was a disappointment. He never did exercises with us during our PT sessions. He gave us instructions on how and what to do but never did them with us—my first lesson in "Do as I say, not as I do." Hypocrite.

"On your feet!" Petty Officer shouted. The class jumped up from the sitting position as we were waiting for the nightly Physical Training class to start.

"Jumping jacks! ARE YOU READY?!" he shouted.

"ALWAYS READY!" the class yelled back, but then there was an interruption.

"Petty Officer! I can't do jumping jacks," a young man in our class said from the back of our formation.

"Why not?" Petty Officer asked.

"Well, last weekend, I went out with some friends to a tattoo shop. They all got tattoos, and I got a piercing."

The class was mumbling and giggling. I knew some of the guys knew what kind of piercing this young man was talking about, but they never said anything.

"What kind of piercing do you have that will stop you from jumping up and down?!" Petty Officer was confused like the rest of us.

"I got a Prince Albert, Petty Officer."

"A what?"

"It's called a Prince Albert," said the young man. As he replied, he moved his hips in a shaking motion, left to right. I could hear little bells or chimes in his shorts. What the hell was that? I thought?

"Aye man, you have to tell me what a Prince Albert is. I have never heard of that." Petty Officer's voice filled with annoyance.

"Petty Officer, I got my dick pierced," the young man said.

You could hear an ant piss on cotton. Everybody and everything got quiet and stood still. Then came the outburst of laughter! It took a little time for all of us to process this moment. I had never heard of someone piercing their delicacies, and I'm sure I was not the only one. The main reason we laughed was because this had to be the stupidest thing we ever heard of a human doing to themselves. Our PT session was cut short that day.

School in Florida was fun. I was, for the first time in my life, on my own and being responsible for my decisions and the consequences that came with them. I lived in an integrated barracks. Each floor was either all female or all male. There was always a watch-stander on duty on each level to watch for Sailors of the opposite coming to visit during the night. The rooms were set up like college dorms. There were two twin beds with a nightstand in between and two desks and a clothing cabinet with drawers against the wall with another nightstand in between them. All the furniture was original light wood. The room furniture reminded me of an old, out-of-date hotel. Everyone had a roommate and a bathroom connected our rooms. With four people sharing a shower, it made for compelling arguments and cleanliness. I was lucky to have the roommate I did.

Enjoli was a short African-American female like me. She wore her hair in a cute pixie cut. She was dark-skinned and had a funny, New York, girlie personality. We loved walking to the Navy Exchange store every payday to purchase the hottest CDs that came out. My CD collection was on point! I loved shoe shopping, and she enjoyed shopping for boyfriends. There was one particular guy Enjoli liked. Every time she saw Chris, she would become anxious.

"Girl, do you see him? The things I would do to him! He is so chocolate and cute!" Enjoli could go on and on, but the way my mind was set up, I did not want to hear about her wanting to fuck him. Show me some pretty girls!

"Let's walk past his table so he sees us. Come on!" she said.

"You are doing way too much! Just go talk to him," I told her, irritated.

"I can't do that. I don't want Chris to think I'm easy." Her thought process made absolutely no sense to me, but whatever. I supported her.

We walked by the table. Chris was sitting with his friends, their leftover food wrappers and drink cups strewn about the table. Enjoli looked in his direction as Chris glanced up. They locked eyes. He smiled at her with the prettiest straight white teeth. There was an undeniable attraction between them. I couldn't take it anymore, so I stopped to speak.

"Chris, hey! My girl wanted to know if you were seeing anybody." I asked. Yep, I'm that friend. If you can't get it done, I will help you.

"Naw, I'm not," he replied. Tell Enjoli she can speak to me. I don't bite."

"Okay, I will be right back!" I took off after Enjoli.

"Why did you walk away?" I asked. "I am trying to make things happen for you! Anyway, Chris said come talk to him."

"He did? What did you say? OMG!" Enjoli exclaimed.

I grabbed her hand and led her to Chris. Little did I know this would backfire on me.

* * *

"Shhhhh, you gonna wake Courtney up," Enjoli said quietly.

I woke up in the middle of the night to Tina Marie's song "Portuguese Love" playing on CD on our shared alarm clock. Hazy and confused, I lifted my head slightly off my pillow, trying to clear my vision. As my eyesight focused, all I saw were two butt-ass naked bodies on top of the bed across from me.

Holy shit! I thought to myself. These jokers are fucking on top of the bed two feet away from me, butt-ass naked! They had no shame. Enjoli was moaning, and Chris was kissing all over her.

What the hell was I supposed to do? I was scared to move, to breathe, to exist.

"Oh my God! We are going to be in trouble if Courtney wakes up, but you feel so good," she said. "Don't stop."

I knew I wasn't going to tell anyone what happened. I didn't want Enjoli and me to both be in trouble for letting a male in our room. I couldn't believe this was happening, and worse, I could not go back to sleep. Instead, I lay there, suffering from this live sex show that was happening in my room. No one would ever believe me if I did say anything.

Soon, it was over. Chris was getting dressed, and he was even kind enough to get Enjoli a wet bath cloth to wash up. She got dressed as well in her pajamas and walked Chris to the door. They kissed goodnight, the door shut, and Enjoli climbed into bed. I finally rolled over, eyes wide open, thinking, Damn, this is the Navy? I never spoke to Enjoli or Chris about that night. To this day, they don't know I was wide awake.

While going through school, I met a guy named Luis Roberto Santiago. He was always the center of attention inside the barracks and outside when all the students would lounge around after class. The girls thought he was the most beautiful thing on earth, and he seemed to agree with their assessment. Luis was going to school for Air Traffic Controller and had been in school for a while. Tall and light-skinned, he had straight black hair that he kept in a faded haircut like black guys with his hairline edged up. His complexion was bronze, but his cheeks were always rosy. He was Puerto Rican from New York, so he had a thick accent that combined the two. Because he was in school so long, he was privileged to wear regular civilian clothes after school and on weekends instead of having to wear uniforms like the rest of us. He always wore baggy jeans with Timberland boots, a gold herringbone necklace with a matching bracelet, and a pinky ring. Luis was like the famous high school senior, and we were the innocent freshmen looking at him in amazement, wanting to be his number one girl. I wasn't impressed with him. There was something about him that made me think he was trying to cover up or prove something. He was trying too hard and doing too much in my opinion, but the young girls fell for him. To my surprise, he somehow fell for me.

"Aye, shorty. It's Kittrell, right?" Luis asked me one day while I was sitting in the lounge waiting for Enjoli to get ready so we could do our afternoon walk around the base.

"If you know, why are you asking?" I said. This was not my first time getting hit on. If it happened once, it was going to repeat the same way every time. He was not slick.

"Damn! Is it like that? I was trying to say hello. HELLO!" and Luis walked away.

Who does he think he is fooling? I can read all through him. He ain't getting this! I thought.

Right after Louis walked away, Enjoli walked around the corner into the lounge.

"Girl, what you think about Santiago?" she said with a smirk on her face.

Now, I know this heffa is not about to make Luis her next victim. We only in school for three weeks! What was she trying to do? Break a record?

"He all right. I mean he cute, but he got too much going on. I know he probably out here sleeping with everybody," I said as I gave her the side eye, hoping she would catch on and see the connection I was trying to make with her and Chris.

"You ought to talk to him," she said. "I don't think he has a girlfriend. He just out here wildin'"

"Whatever. Let's go." I was over the conversation.

As Enjoli and I walked around, I thought about what she had said. Luis was not a bad person. He was having fun. Maybe if I got to know him and we hit it off, I might be happy. Hell, I might have sex and have an orgasm! I still wasn't sexually attracted to men, but I would try just in case something in me changed.

"Enjoli, Imma give Santiago my number," I told her. "I don't know where he is getting stationed though."

"When is the next time you will see him?" she said. "Ask him where he is going before you waste your time."

"If I see him sometime this week, I'll give it to him. If he calls, he calls. If not, oh well. We graduate on Friday. Hopefully, I'll see him before then." I sighed.

The week went by and graduation happened. After graduation, Enjoli and I packed our sea bags and cleaned our barracks room in preparation for inspection before we left. Enjoli was flying out that day, and I had to move into another place for the night and fly out the next day. That was the last time I saw Enjoli, and it would be the first of many friendships that the Navy snatched away from me. As I was walking to my new building for the night, Luis saw me and came over to help me with my bags.

"Kitt! Where are you going?" he yelled.

"I have to move into the other building for the night. I'm flying out tomorrow," I yelled back.

"Let me help you with your sea bag," Luis said as he walked up and yanked it off my shoulder.

"Thanks." Okay, he was kind, and the fact that he ran over to help me when he could have just watched me walk by struggling, pulled on my heart strings.

I checked into my room. It was a hotel room. I had a queen-size bed with the standard floral heavy quilt and blackout curtains to match. It smelled old and musty, but at least it wasn't the barracks!

Luis put my bags down and just stood there looking at me.

"Thank you for helping me. I appreciate it," I said, trying to hint for him to leave.

"Why are you rushing me? You don't like me or something?" he asked.

"I like you. I don't like you, like you. I see you flirting with all those girls. I'm not stupid," I told him. Luis was not going to trick me.

"But where am I right now? I could have still been out there with my boys. I didn't have to help you," he said sarcastically.

Yeah, he got me with that. "You're right," I said.

If you let people do what they want to do, they will show you what they would rather do. Luis put his moves on me that night. I fell for him. We had sex, and nope, nothing happened for me. I continued to try and be a part of the mold that I was supposed to fit in according to the world's eyes. I was still struggling with acknowledgment of my true feelings and who I was truly meant to be. I was a prisoner in my own life trying to find a way to break free. I held on to my secret, trying to get through life the best way I knew how.

CHAPTER NINE

The Start of a Journey

I left Pensacola November of 1999. I took my first leave period for two weeks and spent it with my family. My brother, Michael, was still living at home. He was fifteen years old at the time. Mom finally found a job working for the Greensboro Police Department and was settling in nicely. Two weeks go by fast as hell when you know that is all the time you have. I dreaded having to leave my family, not knowing what my next destination would be. I had never really traveled anywhere outside of visiting family in Virginia, North Carolina, South Carolina, and Georgia. Even then, those visits were two or three days at the most. Here I was, about to be on my own at eighteen, with no parental guidance or discipline, no instruction, no one overseeing me. My security blanket was no more. I was left to fend for myself with the hope that my parents had given me the necessary tools to survive on my own and make the best decisions possible. I was the fruit of their labor.

I arrived at Norfolk International Airport on November 17, 1999. I waited outside the airport with my sea bag and garment bag praying that I would not be forgotten. At this time, there was not a sponsorship program to assist new personnel with transferring to commands. New Sailors were left to figure it out on their own. I received a Welcome Aboard package that contained information for Hampton Roads, information for my command, and a Duty Phone number to call once I arrived in Norfolk. I did not own a cellphone. That was not a thing in 1999. I used a pay phone to call my new command to inform them that I was at the airport. So then, it was a waiting game for them to pick me up. A white van pulled up to the curb and a young man jumped out.

"Are you Airman Kittrell?" he asked.

"Yeah, that's me," I replied.

"How are you doing? Are all these your bags? I'll grab 'em for you."

The Petty Officer picked up my bags and placed them in the back of the van. I hopped in the front seat. I was so nervous.

"Welcome to Virginia," he said sarcastically.

"Why do you say it like that?" I asked.

"Well the weather is wacky, the traffic is fucking terrible, and people in Virginia do not know how to drive."

"What about the command?" I asked, overly concerned about my future.

"Oh, the command is the shit! Yeah! We are like a big ass family! We have about 200 people. It's not bad. We are getting ready to go on deployment in February, so we are doing workups right now. You will more than likely end up in the line shack as all the new kids do."

Work-ups, deployment, 200 people, line shack, what the hell? All I could do was sit and listen to this guy talk about this stuff like it was the best thing since sliced bread. It made for a very long ride.

It was dark by the time we arrived at gate three onboard Naval Air Station Norfolk. It was quiet and cold. The air was still, and it was dark. We pulled up to a dimly lit, old, three-story brick building. It was partially hidden by tall trees whose leaves had long fallen off during the fall weather. Because there was no landscaping, all the leaves covered the ground with patches of dried, brown grass between.

"We are here," Petty Officer said. "This is your barracks. I'll help you get your stuff and bring it in. You need to check in to get a room."

I got out of the van and looked around. Unfamiliar territory at night is so creepy. It looked like a scene from a horror movie. Petty Officer and I walked into the building and up to a desk where a young woman was sitting.

"New check-in?" she asked.

"Yep!" Petty Officer said.

"Fill these papers out. I need your command information and your orders." She handed me a clipboard with different documents attached to it.

I filled them out and handed her a copy of my orders. I received a key to my room and off I went. Petty Officer helped me bring my bags to my room. He was my first impression of the Navy. So far, he was doing a good job.

As I walked the long corridor to my room, the stench of mold, must, and mildew filled my nostrils. I was surprised that the Navy let a building deteriorate this much. The floors were hard and cold with chipped blue tiles. Some of the lights worked in the p-ways, and some didn't. There was a community head on each floor with four showers and six sinks. The building was just dingy.

I entered my room and looked over the two wood-framed, twin beds: one against the left wall and the other directly in front of me, as I opened the door, against the right wall. The room was dark and gloomy. There was a window over the head of my bed which added a little light to the sad place, but not much, because of the massive gold curtains that adorned the sides of the windows. Dark, brown, burlap wallpaper covered the walls. Between the beds were two large, tall wardrobe cabinets with double doors.

This is it, I thought as I walked in with my bags. This was my new home for an indefinite amount of time. I needed a decorator immediately!

"Thank you for helping me. I got it from here."

Petty Officer dropped my bags to the floor.

"I'll see you on Monday. Have a good weekend!" And he left. What was I supposed to do all weekend by myself in a new city, a new home, no car, no friends and definitely no guidance? I was on my own.

I scanned the room and noticed I had a roommate, but she wasn't there at the time. Her belongings looked homely and unkempt. There were clothes lying across her bed as if she'd had a fashion show before she left the room. Her bed was unmade and had a colorful quilt on it with two dirty white pillows. I began unpacking my clothes when I realized there wasn't a bathroom nearby and no television in our room. I was about to be bored out of my mind.

With all my items unpacked and in their places, I decided to take a tour of the building. As I walked down the p-way, I heard noise, chatter, and laughter coming out of a large lounge area. I walked in and saw a lot of young people like me hanging out. It reminded me of school in Florida. They were listening to music, and some were eating fast food at the small tables that were in the room. There were vending machines and couches and a television.

"Hey, girl, what's up?" a female voice said.

I turned around.

"I'm Suzanne. What's your name?"

Suzanne had been in the Navy a little longer than I had, but not by much. She was also living in the barracks and seemed established. She had smooth brown skin, squinty eyes, and her lips were full as if she was always blowing kisses. She was a full-size girl with large breasts and hips. Suzanne was from Tampa, Florida. I could tell she grew up in a rough area because she was aggressive. Shecould bully her way to get whatever she wanted from whomever she wanted and didn't take shit from anybody. She became my very first close Navy friend.

"Hey, I'm Courtney," I replied that first evening. "I just got here tonight."

"Yeah, I can tell. You are walking around like you're scared. It's all good. We all hang out in the lounge. There ain't nothing else to do 'round here. You stationed on a ship?"

At this moment, it hit me. I have to go on a ship! I know this is the Navy, but I just came from an aviation school, my focus was on airplanes, not a ship! Uncle Tim and I talked about ship life and what to expect, but I never gave it a second thought. Out of sight, out of mind mentality. At that moment, my lightbulb went off, and I was going to a ship.

"Ship? No! I am supposed to be checking in at VAW-121. I don't know what that is," I told her.

"Oh, you going to a squadron. That's cool," Suzanne said.

"Are you on a ship?" I asked her.

"Hell yeah, and that shit sucks!" she exclaimed. We burst out laughing.

"I have never seen the ships. I have no idea about that life," I told her.

"Man, there are about 3,000 people on a carrier. You never see the entire ship! It's big as hell! I'll take you to see it if you want."

"Sure," I said.

"Okay. Tomorrow I'm not doing anything. I have a car. Meet me in here at 1300."

"Thanks! Well, I'm going to bed. I'm tired as hell. I'll see you tomorrow." I went back to my room.

Once there, I gathered all my hygiene items to take a shower. My roommate still had not returned, so I hadn't met her yet. I was dreading this long walk down the hall and around the corner to brush my teeth and wash my ass. I finally got to the head, which seemed like a mile walk.

The head was cold, dead, and stale. Old heaters attached to the walls made clicking noises as if the heat was coming on, but there was nothing. The room was painted pale blue and had a hard-blue tile floor. Plastic white curtains covered all the shower stalls. The fixtures on the small, white porcelain sinks were starting to rust. Water carried the rust down the bowl into the drain, leaving permanent brown streaks. This was not my idea of clean. Gwen made me clean and soak everything in Comet and Pine-Sol every Saturday. To see the rust, cold, and cheap white plastic curtains made me want to catch a bus back to Greensboro, take a shower, and come back to Norfolk.

"Just don't touch anything you don't intend to," I told myself.

I walked over to the shower stall and turned on the hot water. I was still wearing my regular clothes but had brought my pajamas and underwear with me. As the water was running, I took off my clothes. All I wanted at that moment was sleep, so showering as quickly as possible was my goal. Naked, I hung my towel on the towel hook and stepped in the shower.

"HOLY SHIITTT!" The water was cold! There was not a speck of heat anywhere. I immediately jumped out and grabbed my towel to wrap myself quickly. As I start to shudder, I thought—This cannot be my life! I'm wet, cold, and naked standing in a cold-ass bathroom without another human being in sight. I started playing with the shower knobs. Maybe they were labeled wrong or backward. I had no luck. But I was not going to bed without a shower. I slowly got back in the shower very meticulously as to not let the water touch my back or my stomach. I stretched out my hand with a washcloth and the soap to lather up. I wanted to cry. I wanted to go home. Little did I know this would be one of many cold showers I would take over the next twenty years.

CHAPTER TEN

A New Beginning

The next day I awoke to the sun trying to pry its way through the heavy curtains that saturated the window. Facing the ugly brown wall, I turned over and saw a body in the bed across from me. Sometime during the night, my roommate must have sneaked in. I sat up, trying to get my bearings and check out my surroundings again. I guess to see if anything had improved overnight. Maybe a television appeared out of nowhere or a piece of paper was slid under the door announcing, "HOT WATER HAS BEEN RESTORED." Wishful thinking.

With my roommate asleep, I quietly opened my wardrobe to get my toothbrush and washcloth for my morning routine. The entire time, all I could think about was my family back home. What was my mom doing? How was my brother acting now that I was out of the house? I was missing them so much. Separation anxiety does not have an age limit. My family was, and still is, a very tight-knit group.

We never miss a holiday, birthday, vacation, or weekend trip. Now, I was alone in a new state, with strangers I was supposed to trust until shown otherwise, and I had no real means of communication. There was no simple email, no social media, no cellphones. It was me, faith, and trust.

I headed back to my room after brushing my teeth and washing my face. The water was still cold. As I walked into the room, my roommate was waking up. I put away my things and started going through my clothes to get dressed for the day. My roommate was a white female. Her hair was sandy blond and cut into a mullet. It looked greasy and thin. She had a thick, masculine build like she should have played football in high school. I could tell as soon as I saw her that she was gay.

"Mornin," my roommate said.

"Good morning," I replied.

My roommate never really engaged in conversation with me, nor did I with her. It was awkward because I knew she was from an entirely different place than I was. Greensboro was a bustling city full of diversity. I was fortunate to be raised to respect others no matter their skin color, the job position they held, or life they led. We are all born into this world with nothing, and we will die with nothing. A lot of people don't think about that. They spend their life being rude, disrespectful and looking down on others, not realizing that when they die, no one will remember them because they never made an impact.

My roommate was from the Midwest. Being around black people was not typical for her, so she didn't know how to respond to me. Because we worked opposite shifts, we were never in each other's way. The morning greeting this day was the only conversation we had.

I walked to the lounge around 1230 to get something from the vending machines. I bought a bag of potato chips and sat on the couch watching TV, waiting for Suzanne to show up.

"Aye girl! You ready?" she yelled as she headed toward the lounge.

"Yeah. I'm just eating these chips. I'm hungry as hell!" I told her.

"We can go get something to eat. I'm hungry too!"

We walked across the street to the barracks parking lot. Suzanne had a teal green, two-door, Honda Civic. It was small and messy on the inside, but to me, at least it was a car. The only thing I had were my two feet. We start driving and she showed me the base and took me to the location of my new command, which was a good way away from the barracks. As we headed to the pier where all the ships moored, I felt myself fill with anxiety and my palms started to sweat. As Suzanne was talking, I couldn't make out anything she was saying to me.

"Where are the ships?" I asked her.

"Girl, you don't see that big-ass ship in front of your face?" she replied.

My eyesight became clear, and all I saw was the color gray. Oh my God! I said silently to myself. "Are you serious? This is the ship?"

"You are stupid. Yes, this is the ship. You okay?" Suzanne said as she laughed at me.

There were three carriers pier-side: USS DWIGHT D. EISENHOWER (CVN 69), USS ENTERPRISE (CVN 65), and USS THEODORE ROOSEVELT (CVN 71). I wanted to cry. I was expected to live on one of these monsters and learn my way around. Learn how to function by myself with no help. This was a huge culture shock for me.

After driving around Norfolk and getting food, Suzanne and I headed back to the barracks. I needed to get my uniform together for my big day. I also wanted to call home and tell my mom about the ships I saw and how amazingly huge they were. I was also starting to miss Luis. I wondered how he was doing in school and if I would ever see or speak to him again. I knew he was putting on an act in Florida. I wanted to get to know the real Luis Roberto Santiago.

***

Luis made an appearance one day at my barracks. It just so happened that he had a friend that was living in the barracks at the time. We crossed paths and our friendship rekindled. We picked up where we'd left off. He was stationed at Naval Station Oceana in Virginia Beach. He soon moved into a studio apartment. Luis was the only familiar and comfortable thing I had in Virginia, so I held onto him. We hung out every chance we could. He was a true friend. When my separation anxiety became too much for me to bear, he offered his car for me to drive home and visit my family. I was so grateful to him for that.

The day came, while I was on my first deployment, when I called Luis to see how he was doing. I wanted to check on my friend, or by then, it was boyfriend. The phone rang and an unfamiliar voice answered.

"Hello?" the voice said.

I was confused. Who the hell was this female answering Luis' phone? My heart started beating fast and I could feel my blood pressure rising.

"Um, may I speak to Luis?" I asked. My voice quavering with anger.

"He is not here. Who is this?" she asked.

"This is Luis' girlfriend for the last six months! Who the hell are you?" I shouted.

"I'm his current girlfriend and he don't want you no more!" she exclaimed. The phone hung up.

This was the very first time I was broken in half. The amount of confusion, anger, disrespect, feeling of losing control, not being in control, was extremely painful. All I could do was cry. I was on a ship in the middle of the Arabian Gulf, calling home to talk to someone who I invested my emotions in, who I considered to be a part of my life, who I trusted, and he betrayed me with not a care in the world.

Young adults who are living on their own for the first time are not prepared to handle situations of betrayal, disloyalty, broken heart, and emotional death. I was emotionally torn up, not eating or sleeping, just wanting to know why Luis turned on me. I wanted an explanation. I wanted closure. But the Navy doesn't care about your personal life. You suck it up, whatever you are going through, show up to work on time and do your job.

***

"How are you getting to work tomorrow?" Suzanne asked me as we walked toward the barracks.

"I don't know," I replied. "I was thinking about calling the duty driver to pick me up."

"They are not going to pick you up. I leave around 0630 to go to the ship. I can drop you off before," she told me.

"Oh man! Thank you so much. I owe you."

"Don't worry about it. You give me gas money and we are straight!"

"I got you," I said, and laughed with relief.

The next morning, my alarm went off at 0500. The room was cold and dark. My roommate was not home from work yet. Her schedule was Sunday through Thursday because she worked nights. I slowly dragged myself out of bed. I could not sleep because of my anxiety of having to check into a command I knew nothing about, thinking about making sure my uniform was squared away, getting to work on time, and what was going to happen. I dragged myself down the hall for my usual morning routine. Then, I dressed in my Winter Dress Blue uniform. I grabbed my big yellow manila envelope to make sure I had all my documents that would probably be needed. Off I headed to the lounge to meet Suzanne.

"Morning girl! You look clean in your uniform," she said when she saw me. "You ready?

"Yep. I'm ready. I think I have everything. I don't know what my command is going to need, but I guess I will find out when I get there," I replied.

Suzanne dropped me off in front of a big yellow building. I could hear the sound of support equipment starting in preparation for the day's flight schedule. The sun was slowly peeking up over the horizon, emanating an orange glow. I entered the building through a glass door. The hustle and bustle of the morning was happening from Sailors coming on shift.

People were walking up and down the halls in blue coveralls holding green books. I spotted a set of stairs to my right and decided to go upstairs. Once upstairs, I saw a sign over a door that read, "ADMINISTRATION," and walked in.

"Good morning," said a Petty Officer working behind the counter.

"Good morning," I replied.

"Are you checking in with us?" he asked.

"I think so. I have my papers here. I don't know all what you need." I handed him the big folder.

"Okay. Let's see here. I need your orders so I can make a copy and stamp them showing that you did show up on time," he said.

I stood there, knowing I had a weird, uncomfortable smile on my face, the same smile two strangers give each other walking down the street. I could have made small talk, but I didn't know anything about the Navy, so I just stood there awkwardly. He handed me back my papers and said, "Um, you are supposed to be checking into VAW-121, but they are not here right now. They are on detachment for two weeks." How was my command gone for two weeks? My duty driver didn't tell me that when he picked me up from the airport. I was confused.

Three days went by with me showing up to the Admin office to muster. The Commanding Officer walked into the office and saw me sitting there. He was an amiable older gentleman wearing a green flight suit, and I could tell by the response of the Sailors when he walked in the office, that he was well respected, and he reciprocated the same respect.

"Good morning! Are you new to the command?" he asked me with enthusiasm in his voice.

"Yes, sir. She just got here. I think she is supposed to be checking in," said a young woman I had not seen before.

"Okay. No worries," said the CO. "Come with me. I can check you in. I have some free time on my schedule." Off I went with him to his office.

The Commanding Officer is the head of a command. They are responsible for the day-to-day functions of their command, operations, and personnel. There is also the Executive Officer, who usually deals more with the personnel side and reports to the Commanding Officer, and last, the Command Master Chief, who is the liaison between all the enlisted personnel and commissioned officers at a command.

I walked into the CO's office. A living treasure chest of his career, it had various large, framed photos of the airplanes he flew. US Naval history books sat on his coffee table and were stacked neatly on his bookshelf, and thousands of challenge coins, which are a vast military collector's item, were lined across his desk and displayed on multiple wooden coin holders. I was enamored.

"Let's see. Airman Kittrell, where are you from?" he asked me as we sat on his couch.

"Greensboro, North Carolina, sir," I said. I was trying to make a good impression. I sat up straight—hands on my lap. My military bearing was on 100. The first impression is always the last impression.

"How far is that from here?" he asked.

"About four hours," I replied.

"Okay so close to home. Awesome! I have some friends from North Carolina," said the CO. People always want to relate to you somehow, like it will suck the awkwardness out of the room. If you are gay, they once had a gay friend. If you are black, their best friend is black. People pick up on that, and it can be very annoying. I believe people do this because they are trying to show you that they are okay with you being gay or black, but really, who cares? I'm not looking for acceptance from any stranger I have ever met. As the CO looked at my orders, he paused. "Wait, you are supposed to be at VAW-121. We are VAW-120," he told me.

"I know, sir. The Petty Officer in Admin said my command was away and will not be back for two weeks, so he made me show up with y'all until they come back." I was trying to explain myself. My first impression was on the line. Now, I was starting to look incompetent as hell, and I was getting mad.

"Okay. Hold on. They are not underway. Your command is next door. Have you been mustering with us all week?" he asked.

"Yes, sir. I was doing as instructed." I was not going to get in trouble. I turned that table around quickly. I was instructed to be here, so that is what I did. Little Airman

Kittrell knew how to follow directions, except for that one time in boot camp, but it was well worth it!

"Let's go back to Admin," he said.

The CO and I walked back into Admin. "I need someone to take Airman Kittrell over to the Bluetails," he said. "She is not supposed to be here. Who told her VAW-121 was not home?"

I could hear the aggravation in the Commanding Officer's voice. Hell, I was aggravated as well. I was already under a lot of stress and anxiety not knowing what was coming. I was given wrong instructions that I now had to clear up because it looked like I didn't know what I was doing. No one spoke up.

"I'll take her over, sir," said the same female who told him I was checking in.

"Thank you," he said and left.

The young woman walked me next door. I entered, and there was that hustle and bustle of people, blue coveralls, and green books. It was a repeat from the beginning of the week when I was checking in at the wrong command. I was led upstairs to Admin. I handed over my orders yet again.

"Airman Kittrell?" a First-Class Petty Officer behind the desk asked.

"Yes, that's me," I replied.

"It's about time you showed up! I was about to mark you UA! We have been looking all over for you! You were supposed to check in three days ago! Where have you been?" He was upset.

"I was next door. I walked in the wrong building, and the Petty Officer there told me y'all were not home. Y'all were on detachment for two weeks, so he made me muster with them." I could tell by the look on his face he did not believe anything I said. What a way to start my new life. Welcome to my new home.

CHAPTER ELEVEN

I met my first command with tests, trials, and tribulations. I was eager and hungry to learn what I needed to be successful. I did not have any mentors, especially females I could look up to. There was no one to guide me. I was thrown to the wolves to figure it out and do my best to stay alive.

VAW-121, also known as the Bluetails, was an all-male command. When I arrived in November 1999, they had just started receiving female Sailors. The attitude throughout the command from all the males stationed there was, of course, very chauvinistic, very insulting, and very demeaning. The strong disdain for females being allowed to serve saturated the air. The men believed that we females were not worthy of wearing the uniform, and that we would never be equal to them no matter how hard we tried. Female service members sacrifice the same if not more. Still, we will never equate to our male counterparts. For us, the pressure is twice as hard.

We have to daily prove that we are not weak, no matter how tired and broken we are inside. We have to prove that we know just as much about our jobs if not more and fight for a chance for our voices to be heard. We are looked down upon the moment we want to have an all-female mentorship program. Complaints such as reverse sexism and discrimination are expressed, but because of the ignorance and blinders on the male servicemembers, it wouldn't be this way if they stopped to mentor the females the same way they do the junior males. Instead, they seek out other, more senior females to handle the responsibility of correcting, mentoring, and dealing with issues regarding women because the males don't know how and don't want to do it.

Because I didn't have a rate or job, I was assigned to the Line Division, which, in a squadron, is where new personnel are assigned to complete the "dirty" taskings on the aircraft. We were responsible for the fuel, cleanliness, launching, and recovery of the aircraft, quick flight inspections, and moving the aircraft in and out of the hangars.

"Oh shit! Look y'all! We got a girl in the shop," said Airman Smith. Smitty, as everyone in the shop called him, had been in the Navy for three years when I showed up. I saw that he was the smart-ass of the shop and was going through the motions, not wanting to achieve anything. He just wanted a paycheck on the first and fifteenth. Very tall and lanky, Smitty had the smoothest brown, flawless skin with the prettiest black curly hair. He looked like he was a player in high school and the girls were attracted to him. I was not impressed. All the guys in the shop turned and looked at me as I walked in with my check-in paperwork.

"She ain't gonna make it! I don't know why, all of a sudden, there are girls in this command. Now, we have to be sensitive so we don't make them cry," said another guy in the shop.

What did I just walk into? I thought to myself. Are they serious?

"Aye! Hold it down and shut up!" said the supervisor.

"Where are you coming from, Airman Kittrell?" the supervisor asked me in front of everyone. I was so damn nervous. The shop was like a dungeon. It was dirty, and it smelled like gasoline and oil. Some of the chairs in the room had missing armrests. The chairs looked as if they had been blue once upon a time but turned black over the years from dirty uniforms.

"Bootcamp, Petty Officer," I responded.

"I know that, smart-ass! Where are you from? Where did you live?" he asked in an aggressive tone.

"Oh! I'm from North Carolina," I answered.

I could sense that this was going to be a struggle. I had never been discriminated against. I didn't know what it felt like, but I was starting to understand. The closest thing to discrimination I ever encountered was an eight-year-old white boy calling my brother a nigger on the playground at Hester's Childcare back home. It angered me so much that I wanted to knock his ass out! I found the closest object I could, which was a tree branch, and I hit him upside his head. We were both pulled into the director's office.

Our parents were called. My stepdad showed up, furious because he didn't know the full story. All he knew was that I hit a kid with a tree branch and cut his face. Once the entire story was told, the white boy was spanked in front of us, and the daycare expelled him. I knew from that moment, that I would always stand up for fairness and also not let anyone mess with my brother!

"Here you go," Smitty said, as he threw me some bags with plastic pieces in it. I sat there looking at the bag, with no clue about what it was.

"I'll help you put it together," said Airman Nunez. Airman Nunez was from Belize, an older black male with a very soft and pleasant personality. He was in the Line Division for a while, and like me, he didn't have a rate either.

"Thank you," I said softly.

"Naw, man! Fuck that! They want to be treated equal, make her put her shit together! I ain't doing nothing for no bitch that come up in here," shouted Airman Smith.

I was in shock! What the hell was wrong with this dude?! All I did was show up, and he was determined to make me feel like shit.

"Shut up, Smitty! Why you always got something to say," said Airman Nunez. "Don't worry about him. He just mad he been in the shop for three years, and he doesn't have a job!"

That outburst from Airman Smith was my very first introduction to my work center. Going through all that emotion during my check-in set the tone of the command for me. I knew that I was up against the grain. If I wanted to make it, I was going to have to deal with a lot of bullshit. I needed to keep my head low and swing every chance I got. I vowed that, from that point on, I was going to complete every task assigned to me better than the next man in that shop. Smitty was my motivation. The more you hate on me, the harder I am pushing! That was my mantra.

My work ethic gained the attention of our supervisor and the Chief. In six months, I was informed that I was taking over the night shift as a supervisor. I was in a state of shock. I was now responsible for all the inspections, fueling, and personnel on nights.

"What the fuck, man! How the hell she gets night check supervisor, and I been here for three years?" Smitty shouted. This shit ain't fair!"

I chuckled to myself because this young man could not see his faults through his hatred of me and all I represented to him. Sometimes you have to move in silence. When you focus on your swim lane, the effort you put in will pay off. When you start to focus on other people's swim lanes, you will get sidetracked and slow down, providing an opportunity for others to swim pass you. My focus was on my swim lane.

December 1999, my command conducted an under-way period onboard USS DWIGHT D. EISENHOWER. It was my very first time being on a ship. It took me a long time to learn how to navigate through the narrow p-ways, how to make a shower bag with all my hygiene items to ease the transition from my rack to the shower. I had to learn how to walk about when the ship would rock back and forth without hitting my shin on the knee-knockers. My ultimate lesson was how to overcome my seasickness. Being on a ship and working out of small office spaces did strengthen the bond between my shipmates and me. I was taken out of the Line Division to help and also learn Aviation Administration. I was placed in Maintenance Control, which is the heartbeat of a squadron. All maintenance operations and planning take place in Maintenance Control. We work 24 hours a day and seven days a week. There no "off" days onboard a ship. I was quickly trained.

"Airman Kittrell! Airman Kittrell! Get up! What are you doing?" asked AZ2 Delarosa.

I slid back the blue curtains that adorned my top rack and saw AZ2 standing in front of me with her green jersey and blue utility pants, hair neatly styled, and makeup flawlessly applied.

"Why are you up?" I asked her. "It's freaking Saturday. I'm trying to sleep in. Go away!" I snatched my curtains closed but heard them open back up.

"What the hell? You do know we work seven days straight on the ship, right?" she asked me, trying not to laugh.

"Wait, what?! I said shocked. "What the hell? You mean we work seven days straight on the ship?" I felt like I was deceived! Seven days straight with no break? I did not read that in my contract!

"Girl, get your ass out of your rack! You are already late," said Delarosa.

I lay back down on my pillow, thinking, Yep, I'm done when this contract is up. I can't work seven days straight. Fuck my life. All the comforts of life that I knew were gone. I was not ready for the adjustment needed in the Navy. That underway period, I learned a lot about the inner workings of a squadron, such as who runs the squadron (which is the Maintenance Master Chief), and what roles everyone played according to their rank.

I was making it through my first tour. I adapted to my surroundings. I began to love what I was doing, and it was evident that I was doing it right. I learned how to be outspoken at the right times and sit back and observe during other times. AZ1 Sandra Broadwater took me under her wing. She was my very first mentor without my knowing it. Soon, I was qualified as a Plane Captain and working permanently in Maintenance Control. I chose to be an Aviation Administrator and quickly advanced from E-3 to E-5 during my tour at VAW-121. There were hardships in having to know how to demand respect and to be treated with fairness without being disrespectful. It is all in how a person carries themselves, what they are willing to entertain, and their work performance. There were days I wanted to cry and go home, but I knew giving up was not an option.

One night, I walked into Maintenance Control. The night check Chief, Senior Chief Woolsey, wanted to know how many people we had in our shops. I knew I wasn't supposed to let anyone go home early. I would rotate my people out when I could so we could take a break now and then. I would always stay. I knew if I took care of my people, they would take care of me.

"Kittrell, how many people you got in your shop?" Senior Chief asked me.

I froze. I didn't want to lie, but I didn't want to tell the truth either and get my face shot off. I might get fired, and no one would trust me anymore. I stood there silently.

"Goddamnit, girl! How many people do you have? You don't understand English?" he shouted.

"Senior, I had to let one person leave. They had an emergency." I told him the truth, and I lied at the same time. There was no emergency, but I did let one of my guys go home early.

"What the fuck you do that for? Didn't I tell you no one leaves without coming through me?"

I wanted to drop dead on the spot. I had messed up trying to look out for my people.

Senior Chief Woolsey gave me the business that night. That was the first time I broke down so bad that I wanted to walk out of work and go UA.

"Man, fuck this place!" I yelled as I walked down the hall toward my shop.

I grabbed my keys. I'd had enough, so I was leaving. The harassment, lack of trust in my capabilities, the stress of being away from my family and having no support was burning me out. It was a lot to take on at nineteen years old. I couldn't do it anymore.

As I walked out into the parking lot, crying, I heard chatter coming from the gazebo that was used as a smoke pit. We mostly just hung out in there when work was slow. I heard footsteps run up on me as I approached my car.

"Kittrell! Hold up! What's wrong?" called out someone as he got closer.

I turned around and Airman Smitty was looking at me with a level of concern I had never before seen from him.

"Fuck this place! Fuck you! I'm so over being treated like shit! I'm tired of everyone thinking that I can't do my fucking job because of me either being black, a female or both! Leave me alone!" I yelled at him.

I broke down sobbing uncontrollably. Smitty grabbed me and hugged me tightly.

"Kitt, don't leave. We need you," he said. "Look. I know I am an asshole. I shouldn't have said the things to you that

I said. I apologize. I got your back. You are doing a good job, and all the guys like you. They don't show it, but we talk when you're not around," he said.

I was in shock. Never in a million years did I ever think that Smitty would be the one to put my pieces back together. He will never know how much this night affected my leadership and me. It taught me that no matter how much you feel like giving up, someone somewhere is depending on you for something. I mattered to my shop. Even though they never showed it, I truly mattered. My early years in the Navy brought me so many opportunities that I will never forget. I was getting a chance to see parts of the world that others could only dream about: Puerto Rico, Portugal, Italy, Bahrain, Dubai, Croatia, Jerusalem, Bethlehem, Italy, Spain, and scores of places in America. I knew I had something special. Despite all of the hard times, the lessons and memories of the good times would see me through.

CHAPTER TWELVE

New Friends

I made a lot of new friends from different backgrounds. I always had a pleasant personality and I treated everyone with respect, thanks to a solid upbringing. It was exciting and scary at the same time. I never hung around or befriended anyone who wasn't American. Greensboro was diverse, but I lived in a predominantly black area of the city. My elementary school was majorly white, but middle and high school were all black. All my friends were American. The Navy opened my eyes to different cultures and countries that I never knew existed and friends I never knew I would have.

AK3 Brandy Borowski was my first white friend from Polka, West Virginia. Brandy was short, thick, and had the bubbliest personality. Her skin was milky white, and her reddish-blond hair enhanced her green eyes. She attracted attention because of her personality. We got to know each other during the periodic underways on the ship and during detachments. We returned from deployment when Brandy became pregnant. We were living in a new barracks at Naval Station Norfolk. She was stressed out about having to move out into town by herself. I felt terrible for her, so I offered to move out into town with her.

"Courtney, you're gonna do what?" Mom exclaimed. "Who is the girl? You don't know her like that to be roommates!"

"Mom, stop worrying. She is not bad. Besides, we are roommates now, and she is okay. What difference does it make? I'll have my first apartment, and you can come to visit!" I said. The thought of having my apartment was exciting. I had never paid bills, but whatever. I would figure it out.

Brandy and I moved to an apartment complex in Virginia Beach, Virginia. It was a beautiful complex across the street from a hospital and close to the major highway, fast food restaurants, and shopping outlets. It was a two-bedroom, two-bathroom, apartment with living room, dining room, and kitchen with a dishwasher, all for $600 a month. That was $300 between us. What was more amazing about this apartment was that it was down the street from AK2 Daniel K. Aquilano.

Daniel was pure Italian. He had black hair that made his piercing blue eyes stand out. Those eyes were the first things you noticed about him. He was kind and generous. He knew his job at work and was a favorite of the Maintenance Master Chief. Everybody knew AK2. Soon, we started dating, and people couldn't believe it. Again, I was trying to cover up my true urges by dating a guy. I was attracted to Dan's personality. He was outgoing and a people person. He had a quirky sense of style but it didn't bother me. When Brandy and I moved into our apartment, I would spend most of my time at Dan's. We tried to keep our relationship on the low at work, but that is hard to do when you hang out on the weekends with the same people you work with. Our relationship was short-lived when he transferred to another command out of Virginia. I was back to just me.

Brandy was progressing through her pregnancy. Her mother wasn't too fond of her being pregnant, and the baby's father wanted nothing to do with her or the baby. All she had was the other pregnant females and me at her new command.

"Hey, Court! These are my friends from work," Brandy said. "They came to hang out with me. Hope that's okay."

I just walked into the door of the apartment after a long day at work. It was eleven o'clock at night. I wanted to shower, watch television, and relax. I was not expecting to see three additional pregnant females in the apartment when I came home, and I was immediately pissed.

"Whatever, Brandy," I said as I walked to my bedroom.

I could hear them laughing and sharing stories of their pregnancy and how their boobs were swollen and leaking milk, how they were constipated and wanted to sleep. I kept thinking damn, is this what young females do? Have sex, get pregnant and be a single mother? Then form support groups for therapy sessions? I thought about my pregnancy at the age of sixteen. Here I was at the age of twenty-one, and I knew I was not ready for a baby. Again, things happen for a reason. I knew my mom was looking out for me because she knew what was best for me, but emotionally I was struggling.

Living with Brandy became difficult. She was not a bad person; I was just too independent and needed to be on my own. We fell out, and I eventually moved. I took with me all the furniture and kitchenware we had that was given to me by my family. Brandy was left with her bedroom set. I moved into a small, one-bedroom apartment in Norfolk, VA. During my time with Brandy, I met a man named Michael Greely through my friend Shameka back at home.

Michael Deshawn Greely was from Winston-Salem, North Carolina. He grew up in a big family and was the baby boy. His father was deceased, and his mom was indeed the matriarch. Mike would drive to Virginia every weekend to spend time with me. He was a nice guy, about 5'8" with coffee-brown skin. He wore prescription gray-colored contacts and was never without a ball cap that matched every outfit he wore. Mike had full lips and a lined-up black mustache. My dad told me Mike reminded him of Shane Mosely, the boxer. Mike loved fast cars and motorcycles. He drove a low, four-door Honda Accord that was custom-painted a bright purple. He re-configured his car to include a television in the dashboard, and headrests. He also included custom rims and exhaust. It was indeed an eye-catching vehicle. He also had a customized motorcycle that was lengthened and sat lower than most bikes. It was orange and blue, and it was Mike's most valuable prize.

We dated for a while. Mike loved artwork and drawing. He had a degree working with Fiber Optics and was struggling to find a job. He still lived with his mother in North Carolina so what money he made from selling artwork or doing home repairs, he saved in the hopes of moving out and starting a life for himself. My friends began to accept him as part of their family. We did couples dates, but there was still a void in me. Something was missing. From the looks of it, I had it all—a caring boyfriend, a steady job, a paycheck, an apartment, a car. I was successful so far in my life, but I was not happy.

Mike developed feelings for me faster than I did for him. I don't think I had feelings for him at all. He would tell me he loved me, and I would brush it off by saying, "Boy you crazy!" I couldn't repeat those words to him, but I still hung around and allowed him in my life because I was searching for acceptance and needed to have support from somebody, anybody. I went through the motions of life and the expectation of a man and woman. I appreciated his traveling to Virginia every weekend to visit with me. I felt if that was what he wanted to do, then okay. I never asked him to come to see me. I wasn't that serious about us, but he was.

"Courtney," Mike stopped in his tracks as we were walking along the sidewalk on New Year's Eve at Waterside in Norfolk. We had been drinking and partying through the evening, and it was close to midnight. People were lined up on the balcony of one of the restaurants that overlooked the water and into Portsmouth.

"What?" I said, squinting my eyes as I felt the effects of all the drinks I had consumed.

"I don't want to be with anyone else. Will you marry me?" Mike asked, as he got down on one knee. At that moment, in my head, I was running as fast as I could down the street. In reality, I was tipsy and trying to figure out why he was kneeling.

"SAY YES!" a voice yelled out from the balcony. "Yes," I said.

Cheers and screams were echoing from the buildings. Mike got up and hugged me as I stood there limp. What had I done? He grabbed my hand, and we walked down the waterway. He was smiling the entire time, and I was confused. It was too late to turn back now. I couldn't hurt his feelings. Besides this was the way adult life was supposed to be, right? I was to be grown, married, two kids—o-one boy and one girl. I was doing what society said I should do, but it was not what I wanted.

I was silent for the rest of the night. How in the hell do I get out of this? I later found out that Mike spoke with my mom about marrying me. She approved. I was kind of upset about that because I was not ready. I did not want to have decisions for my life made for me by other people. I didn't know how to love myself and be comfortable in my own skin. Now I was expected to love a man unconditionally and be his wife. There were too many pressures on me at that time and I was young. Again, who could I talk to? Who would listen? My life was changing before my very eyes and I felt as though I had no control over what was happening. I was living my life trying to please others and losing myself at the same time. All I could do was pray for strength and a sign from God to make it all better.

CHAPTER THIRTEEN

Leadership Development

My first command, VAW-121, would start me on a leadership and growth path that would mold me without my knowing it. Leadership in the world is a big deal. No matter what job, field, school, or life a person has, leadership is placed somewhere between to help achieve the next level. There isn't one form of leadership that works for every single person on the planet. It is not something that can be taught. Some people are born into this world motivated and hungry, burning with desire to be a blessing not only to themselves, but to others around them. They are compassionate and caring. They embody patience and understanding.

We all begin as seeds, as children. It takes water from our families, our communities, and our education system to ensure we have proper nourishment, and with that, we continue to grow. Some of us are lucky to have been watered by amazing people throughout our lives. Others are not so lucky and have been stunted because of whatever life circumstances they endured, so they stop growing all together as leaders. Their development is cut short.

Airman Timmons checked onboard the command. He was a young, black boy trying to find himself as most do when they initially join the service. He was of average height, had a light build, dark skin and wore thick black-rimmed glasses. He was mild tempered, and I could tell he didn't take life too seriously. Assigned to the line division as well, I got to know Timmons. At the time, our Leading Petty Officer was AM1 Marcantel. AM1 was a short, white male. He had a pink complexion, with little brown freckles that consumed his face. His hair was red, and he wore a thick red mustache that matched. AM1 was all work, no play. What he said was what we did. We executed and reported back for the next tasking when we were given taskings to complete, never questioning anything. We were a well-oiled machine.

One day, Airman Timmons was re-assigned to work in the First Lieutenant division. He was in charge of cleaning, mopping, taking out the trash, stripping and waxing the deck, etc. I don't quite remember what Airman Timmons did to be removed from line division. I do know that he was in trouble, and AM1 Marcantel had had enough of his behavior.

"Timmons, you have to remember this. No matter what you do, your first impression is always your last impression. You will have to kiss 1,000 babies and save the world once you mess up in a squadron. Even after you do all that, they will still remember that one time you messed up!" I told him one afternoon when I was checking on him.

It was on my heart and mind to make sure he was okay. I don't know where that conversation sprung from. I don't know why or how at a young age I was able to form my thoughts and articulate what I told Airman Timmons. I would forever remember this as my very first mentoring session with a junior Sailor before the Mentorship Program began throughout the Navy. It set me on my path.

Leadership development is needed at every corner, from teachers to CEOs of major corporations. You cannot make a herd of cattle go in a particular direction if there is no one to lead them. A leader needs to be in the front guiding, protecting, and keeping their followers out of harm's way. Nowadays, people don't lead for the betterment of their followers. They lead for the betterment of their egos. It is always easy to blame someone for something when it does not get done because we don't want to take responsibility. Passing the buck to the person below you takes the burden out of your hands, but did you train the person below you to understand their job tasking? Did you lead them and guide them, making sure they were set up for success, or did you throw them a curveball and hope they would catch it. Too often, I see situations where leadership will pass the buck to the next person so they don't get in trouble and allowing them to keep their ego intact. It is a problem.

Leadership encompasses the good and the bad. A true leader will never pick and choose when to be a leader because they understand both sides of the coin and are mature enough to accept positive and negative outcomes. Leaders are supposed to be humble servants. We are to serve, protect, and take care of those we are leading as well as learn from them. You cannot be a leader if you don't know how to follow. When I mentor junior Sailors, I give them my four thoughts on leadership:

Leadership is not 100 percent correct. There are a lot of leadership books available to all who want to make a difference in the world, at home, or in their careers. People are unique and require different motivational tools to move them along in life. A kid growing up in Nebraska, working cornfields, playing high school sports, maintaining the honor roll at school, will not have the same motivational requirements as the kid from the inner-city streets in Chicago, growing up with the bare minimum to eat, poor grades at school, and a broken family life.

A different leadership style is needed to get through to these various individuals. A leader must tailor their style to those they are leading. The only way to become successful is to KNOW who you are leading. Step outside the crystal palace and understand your followers so you will know why they think the way they do and what drives them. Everyone has a story.

Leadership is uncomfortable. A good leader will draw in people from all walks of life and different backgrounds. People navigate toward and trust those who radiate positivity; those who can empathize and are willing to share their time. With that, can often come situations that require individual guidance that may be out of a leader's comfort zone. A leader may get a confession about a violent act or thought, he or she may have to deal with a domestic dispute, the loss of a follower's infant, the death of a loved one, etc. The list can go on for years. As a person dedicated to others, a leader will step in regardless of their personal beliefs and feelings and provide the necessary resources to that individual.

Leadership is unappreciated. No one is going to thank you daily for leading them to the water for that cold drink, so don't expect it. The feeling of accomplishment for the leader is seeing the smile on the follower's face after they have drunk the water, and then seeing the follower bring more people to the water to get their taste, and the cycle continues. Just know that if you are doing well and leading well, your "Thank you" will be that promotion your follower receives, or the recognition, or a hot cup of coffee someone poured for you.

Leadership is not fair. There are times in a leader's life when decisions have to be made. These decisions have to be made with the followers' lives taken into account. Two people are in trouble. Person A has a family and has been at his place of duty for ten-plus years. Person B is young, single and has been at her place of duty for five years. Both are in trouble for DUI. When making decisions, information is only on a need-to-know basis. Junior personnel don't need to know every single thing that has taken place behind the curtain. Leaders are the ones who have been dealing with continuous issues from these individuals. When the time comes to separate one of them, Person A is separated from service. Person B is allowed to continue her duty even though both were in trouble for the same violation. This is when leaders have to deal with, understand, and explain in as little detail to junior personnel the thought process, because it looks unfair to the unknowing eye. Person A has been in ten years, but this is not his first DUI nor is it his second. He has been through treatment and failed. Yes, he has a family. No, his wife doesn't work, and the children are in private school. It looks unfair. This is Person B's first offense. She is twenty-one, and it was her birthday. On the outside looking in, they both should have received the same punishment. On the inside looking out, the decision was fair and just. A leader needs to understand the perception of fairness. Communication is essential.

As a Chief, we are humbly asked to face challenges and accept diversity. Many forget the first line of the Chief's Creed because we only recite it once a year when new Chiefs are pinned. The creed is a reminder of the expectations of all Chiefs and can be applied to anyone in a leadership position. Unfortunately, there are occasions where a person does not understand the meaning of leadership. No matter how hard they are mentored, they continue to do what they want, and their Sailors are threatening to complain about working in a hostile environment. When issues like that arise, I always refer to that Chief as an E-7. I will never respect them as a Chief because they should know better.

I had terrible leaders in my career, and they were the leaders that taught me the most. In both situations, I learned valuable lessons that kept me correct throughout my leadership path. Every leader is different and is molded by different hands, so don't expect everyone to lead the same.

I vowed to always to train, mentor, and guide anyone who asks. I have also befriended so many leaders with stories of their struggle and how they rose to their positions despite the negativity and hate. I was put into uncomfortable situations where I struggled as well, but through that struggle, I grew, I accomplished, and I promised to always reach back for those standing behind me.

CHAPTER FOURTEEN

Love Again

transferred to a new command in November 2003. I was a Petty Officer Second Class and doing well for myself. I felt like I had everything in my life under control. Mike and I were still in a relationship. I was not 100 percent dedicated, but Mike was a good guy, and I could not bring myself to hurt his feelings. A Justice of the Peace married us in Virginia Beach, VA. So much for the beautiful white wedding dress, bridesmaids, and honeymoon. I felt so incomplete because that was not what I wanted. I was happy, but I was not pleased. I was living my life for others and not myself.

My new command, Commander, Naval Air Forces Atlantic, was a staff job. I had regular working hours that allowed me a lot of free time in the afternoon after work. A co-worker talked to me about volunteering at Mount Trash-more YMCA. His wife worked there, and she coordinated different events where volunteers were always needed. I thought this was a good plan. It gave me something to do in the afternoons. Mike had a second shift job and would come home around eleven at night, so I had plenty of time to stay busy.

"Hey. What's your name?" Tera asked me.

"I'm Courtney. I just started working here. I was volunteering but decided to get a part-time job since I was here so much," I told her.

"Aww, that cool! Welcome to the YMCA," she said. "Do you go to school 'round here?"

"Naw, I'm in the Navy. Going on five years," I responded.

"Oh, hell naw! I couldn't do it. People are yelling at you in boot camp. Telling you what to do," she said.

"People tell you what to do here. What's the difference? Everybody has somebody they have to answer to," I replied.

"True story. I didn't think about that," Tera said. We laughed hard together.

Tera Pica was 5'8, light skinned, and she had an athletic build. She was a basketball player in high school and loved sports. She worked in the fitness area of the YMCA and was very outgoing. Her personality was infectious. She had full pink lips and wore a short, black, curly, pixie haircut. Mixed Puerto Rican and white, she had very urban mannerisms. I was in love.

The moment I met Tera, it clicked for me. This was what I wanted. This was what I needed. I felt complete being around her because she got me. We talked about everything under the sun. Our families, how we grew up, our siblings, what we wanted to do when we officially grew up. I wanted to be her friend. I wanted to be more than her friend. There was only one issue we faced. We were both in relationships. Neither one of us was happy, but we didn't want to hurt our partners' feelings. So, we comforted each other when we were at work talking about our issues.

Many times, in life, when adults commit adultery, it is usually with someone they have been around for a long time and with whom they have made an emotional connection. Individuals do not go out into the world looking for someone to sleep with, but they do go into the world like magnets, attracting what their hearts desire. An emotional connection is deep. Having someone who understands your sadness, your hunger, your pain, and your wants is a human need. We want to be understood and feel needed. We want to feel connected to someone who cares and who can relate back. Once the emotional connection is made, a relationship is born.

"I don't know what I'm going to do. Tonya always argues, and I'm tired of listening to her bitch about the same shit! I can't catch a break. I can't do anything right," Tera said one day while I was working the membership desk.

"How long have y'all been together?" I asked her.

"Three years. I moved out here with her from Eugene, Oregon," she replied. "I met Tonya through friends. We started a relationship, and then she got a job out here. I followed her here."

"Oh, gotcha," I said.

"What about you? You all married and shit. Having sex every night. How's that going?" Tera asked in a smart-ass way.

"Who is having sex every night?" I said. "Getting married was a mistake. I can't bring myself to hurt Mike's feelings. We don't have sex at all. He tries, but when he gets off work, I do my best to play sleep, or have cramps, or have a headache, or tell him no. I'm not sexually attracted to him." I hoped she would catch on to what I was trying to say without my saying it.

"Aw damn! That's fucked up!" she said, as she started laughing. I told her the story of how Mike proposed to me, and I was too drunk to know what was happening in that very moment. From there, I was stuck. My mom was happy for me. I didn't want to disappoint her, so I went with the flow.

As time went on, I would be so excited to come home and work another job to see and spend time with Tera. Things began to get serious between us. The first time we kissed, Tera was putting workout towels in the washing machine one night. There was no one around, and I walked into the room she was in. She pulled me aggressively toward her. Of course, I did not push away. She kissed me with her soft pink lips, and I kissed her back. The kissing got deeper and deeper. For the first time, my loins were genuinely excited. My little girl in the boat stood up. I started to get very hot and pulled away from her. I looked her in her eyes and ran out of the laundry area. Is this what I was looking for all these years? Is this what intimacy, sex, and romance are supposed to feel like? I wanted more, but I felt ashamed. I wanted to go back and do it over again, but what would the world think of me? I wanted to strip her clothes off and kiss all over her body and feel her skin against mine, but that was not happening.

I pulled myself together as I walked back to the membership desk to begin closing down the YMCA. My panties were moist, and I could not stop thinking about what had just happened. The feeling of being involved in something so taboo was exhilarating. I was on cloud nine. Tera liked me, and I wanted her. We sneaked around the YMCA every time we worked together, trying to find places to be alone without anyone learning of our relationship. Those around us thought that we had just become close friends. No one was the wiser. I was finally doing what I wanted to do. I had finally found what I was missing. Having all these emotions going through me at the same time both confused me and left me feeling so lonely. I still had no one to talk to about what I was going through in my life. I decided to slide the situation into a conversation with my mom.

"Mom, I have to tell you something," I said.

"What?" she replied.

"Well, I keep having dreams about this girl I work with at the YMCA. I mean sexual dreams! I don't know what to do," I told her. After our kiss, I always had different dreams about Tera. It was overwhelming. I didn't know if I was going crazy or what, but I needed to tell somebody to get a second opinion.

"Well, if Mike were doing what he is supposed to be doing in bed, you wouldn't be having these dreams," my mom told me.

I think that was the most awkward conversation I had ever had with my mother up to that point in my life. I didn't know how to respond to that statement. My mother didn't know anything about my sex life. I never told her how Mike only wanted to have sex with me if I was wearing red, high-heeled shoes. That was the only way he could climax.

I hated it, and I thought it was the weirdest thing ever in life. I didn't tell my mom about anything, and now I was trying to tell her about my feelings for another woman. It was the hardest thing I would ever do, and it came with a price.

"Courtney, your husband is on the phone. He said he thinks he is having a heart attack," said Donna, my membership director.

"What?! Oh my God," I yelled as I ran to the phone. "Hello! Mike what's wrong?" I said.

"I need you to come home now. My chest is tight, and I can't breathe!" Mike said. It sounded like he was crying. He could barely get his words out.

I arrived home in 15 fifteen minutes. I entered our apartment, and my jaw dropped when I opened the door. All my furniture was flipped over like a horrible robbery scene. The armchairs lay on their sides. The cushions from the couch were strewn across the living room. The coffee table was upside down. They television was on in the background. Magazine were scattered, alone with my plant decorations, on the floor.

"What the hell happened?" I asked.

"You know what you did! Who the hell is Tera, and don't lie to me!" Mike said.

At that moment, everything flashed through my mind. I thought about his proposal. I thought about the time he asked me if I was gay when we were in the car coming home from the mall, and I laughed it off. I thought about the first time I saw Tera walk past me in the YMCA and I couldn't stop thinking about her. I thought about how I felt when Tera and I kissed, and I felt so complete, so whole. If I wanted to be free of life's shackles and be truly happy, this was my one chance.

"Mike, I can't do this anymore," I told him. "I can't be married. I'm not happy. Tera has nothing to do with how I feel. I have felt like this since the day we were married but didn't know how to tell you."

"Why Courtney, why?" He slid down the wall in the living room, crying. I was so numb. I didn't know what I was supposed to feel. I didn't know if I should run and hug him. It would not have changed anything. I didn't know if I was supposed to apologize. I didn't feel I should because I was suffering on the inside trying to portray and live a life that was a lie.

I was living to please other people and putting myself last. I was so concerned and worried about what people would think of me that I sacrificed another person's feelings, loyalty, and trust. That was the most selfish thing I had ever done in my life. I stood there and looked at him. I wanted this to all be over. I wanted to fast-forward the pain, the regret, the misery, and the drama that I knew I would endure for an indefinite amount of time. I wanted to fast-forward the shame I felt because I wouldn't be accepted in this lifestyle. I wanted to fast-forward the anger and hatred that I would encounter from his friends and family. I just wanted it all to go away and make it better.

CHAPTER FIFTEEN

Losing to Win

I was at a shallow point in my life after Mike found out about Tera and me. I struggled at work because I was so stressed out dealing with my taboo lifestyle and having to keep it a secret, all the while going through a divorce from a man who loved me. I loved Mike; I just wasn't IN LOVE with Mike. I was upset with myself for breaking him the way that I did, but the milk was spilled. I was dealing with life consequences with no guidance, no one to talk to, no one to trust. Work-life balance is real issue. It is truly difficult for a young person who has no life experience and can't discuss their issues with anyone. I suffered in silence. I couldn't talk about it with anyone because the Don't Ask, Don't Tell policy was in full effect in the Navy. Meaning, the Navy couldn't ask if you were gay, and you couldn't tell anyone you were. If it were found out, you would be separated from the Navy. I was trying to deal with this monstrosity of an issue and not having anyone to guide me made my work performance drop and changed my attitude for the worse.

Mike and I legally separated. Tera and Tonya split up. Mike stayed in our apartment until he could find somewhere to live. I felt obligated to pay the rent and all the utilities because, after all, I caused our marriage to explode. Tera and I moved in with her friend John and his husband. I was so uncomfortable and stressed out. At night I went to John's house because I couldn't go to my apartment where Mike still resided. I felt like I was intruding and being a burden on someone else due to my negligence in handling my affairs. John was more than accommodating. He understood what I was going through. I could openly talk to him about my life, my downfalls, and my disappointments. He was my pressure-release valve, but I still needed to talk to my mother. I needed her to know everything. I wanted her to know everything. I was tired of hiding and not being honest. I wanted to be free.

"Mom, there is something I need to tell you," I told her during one of our casual phone calls.

"What, girl?" she said in her feisty high-pitched voice.

"Mom, Mike and I are separated," I told her.

"What? What happened?" she exclaimed.

"Remember the girl, Tera, I told you about? We are in a relationship," I said.

There was a long uncomfortable silence. I was fearful of what would happen next.

"What do you mean you are in a relationship with her? I can't believe this, Courtney. You are going to ruin your career," she yelled.

"Mom, I'm not going to ruin my career! I know what I'm doing. Who is going to find out? I don't talk to anyone at work about my life. They don't know what I'm going through." I wanted to break down and cry. I was finally getting it off my chest and telling my mother in so many words that I was interested in girls. I couldn't say "gay" because I was still trying to process what I was feeling and going through. Being gay was like having AIDS. When people find out, they will whisper about you when they see you coming. They don't want to touch you because they are afraid they may catch it. They don't want you around because you could spread your disease and beliefs onto others. I didn't want that. I love people. I am a people person. I don't want to be judged because of who I like or choose to have sex with. That is my business. As long as I'm coming to work and doing my job, there should be no concern about my personal life.

"Courtney, do not get kicked out of the Navy," my mom said. "You have come so far."

"I won't, Mom. Stop worrying. I am grown. I am paying my bills with my own money. I don't ask you for anything. I want to live my life." I realized I was almost shouting.

I knew my mother was upset with me. Coming out as a lesbian was not what she wanted for her daughter. I was now an embarrassment to my mother. If her friends asked her, "Gwen how are your daughter and son-in-law doing?" she could not and would not be comfortable saying, "Oh, Courtney and Mike are divorced. She is gay and happy now." I felt like a failure for the first time in my life and didn't know how to handle it.

"Shit! I have two flat tires!" I woke Tera up at 0430 in the morning.

"What? How the hell did that happen?" she asked.

"I don't know. I just went to get in the car and noticed the front passenger tire was flat. I'm going to be late to work! I need to call my LPO," I told her.

Having this flat tire added more stress in my life. I was broke from paying rent and utilities at my apartment. What little money I had left over, I used for Tera and me. I was mentally and physically tired. I was working until ten o'clock at night, closing the YMCA. I was finally able to go to bed around eleven every night and woke up at 0345 in the morning to be at work by 0500. It was draining me. I already messed up by opening up to my mother about what I was hiding. I couldn't fail twice. I swallowed my depression and kept pushing. I smiled every day through the pain of not knowing if my mother would ever talk to me again. I smiled every day as I was dying internally. My smile hid my pain. I didn't want to bring too much light to my situation. I couldn't and didn't trust anyone enough to let them into my personal life. I stayed as strong as I could. I would make it on my own with no one's help.

"Hello? AZ1, I have two flat tires. I will not be at work on time. I'm going to call a tow truck to pick up my car so that I can get new tires." I left a message with my LPO. Car shops don't usually open until 0700, so I had about two hours. I lay down on the bed and went to sleep. When I woke up, it was 0900. That sleep was much needed.

"Crap! I need to call a tow truck," I told Tera as she was getting ready for work. "Why didn't you wake me?"

"I don't know. I didn't know what you were doing today. Don't they give you the day off for stuff like this?" she asked me.

"No. I need to get my tires changed and go to work!" I exclaimed.

I could feel myself getting upset. My heart was beating fast, and I was anxious and nervous. I didn't want to get in trouble. Deep down I knew I wasn't going to make it to work, but I wanted so badly to get there to keep from being questioned about my whereabouts, who I was with, what I was doing, etc. Those questions alone can lead to my chain of command finding out I was gay and kicking me out. I was petrified. My mother told me I was making a mistake. I should have listened. I never made it to work that day. I was so upset and scared. I never called my LPO to keep him updated on what was going on with me. I felt like I was losing the battle, and my life was unraveling. I wanted to give up and not face additional drama, discipline, and anger from anyone else. Mike was stressing me out, my mother wasn't talking to me, and now I had to face my command.

The next day I arrived at work. I was the first one in the office as I usually was. I went about my usual routine of starting the coffee, turning on all the lights, and logging into my computer. It was very quiet. I was having anxiety thinking about the wrath that I was about to endure for not coming to work the previous day. I didn't know who would yell at me first. I didn't care. My life was in shambles, and I was struggling to get it back. The back door to the office opened, and people started coming in. Their voices echoed throughout the cubicles. The sound of combat boots walking across the carpet was making my heart race. I didn't know who was going to show up at my desk.

"Good morning, AZ2! How are you doing today?" said AZ1 Clayton. AZ1 Clayton was a black female like me. She had a caramel complexion and thick, wavy hair that she kept in a bun. She was very soft spoken. Her smile captured you with her slight gap between her front teeth.

"Good morning, AZ1. I'm okay, I guess. I was able to get my tires changed yesterday," I replied.

"Oh, I know. Walk with me for a second," she said. I knew, at that moment, I was in trouble.

I followed AZ1 Clayton into the Captain's office and sat on the couch.

"So, what happened yesterday?" AZ1 asked.

"What do you mean? I told you what happened. I had two flat tires. Car shops don't open until 0700. I laid down and fell asleep. When I woke up, it was 0900. I still had to call a tow truck and wait. By the time I got to the car shop, it was almost noon. It took them almost two hours to change my tires."

"So, you took it upon yourself to not come to work?" she asked me.

"No. We get off work at 1400 every day. Why would I come to work knowing no one would be here?" I said. I was getting frustrated. I didn't need this right now. I didn't want to be there. I wanted to run away and leave everybody behind.

"What else is going on with you?" AZ1 asked me.

"Nothing. I'm fine," I said, as I was becoming more and more agitated. My eyes were starting to well with tears. My nose was tingling. I wasn't fine. I wasn't fine at all. My life was in shambles. I had people around me, but I was so alone.

"No, you're not. Your attitude is out of control, and your work performance is declining. Chief asked me about you the other day. He noticed you were quiet. Not as happy go lucky as you usually are." she said.

At this moment, my floodgates broke and I had a meltdown. I cried and cried. AZ1 Clayton was not ready for that reaction. She ran to close the door for privacy. She fumbled through the Captain's office, looking for tissues. I finally had enough. I needed to release all the negativity from my soul. I needed to let go of all the pain I was holding in. I needed to part ways with the stress I allowed to control me and drag me down. I cried. Not because I was in trouble, but because there was so much I wanted to talk about and share, but I couldn't. I wanted to yell, "I'm gay and need support because I don't know where to turn!" but I couldn't. I wanted my mother beside me at that very moment, but I felt she was ashamed of me. I just wanted to be held and told that everything was going to be okay, that I didn't have anything to afraid of, and that my life was meaningful.

Everyone has a story. A story that they want to share with others but are too ashamed or prideful to. The stories we hold in can do unimaginable damage to one's emotions, daily routine, family bond, marriages, relationships. Some people think when a loved one becomes distant or stops communicating that they are acting funny. The idea is to pressure that person into explaining their feelings. The honest truth is that the more a person is pressured into explaining their emotions, the more that person is going shutdown. A person has to wait until they are comfortable, wait until they are ready, wait until they feel they have a trusted listener before they will talk. Give them space.

Support them. Let them know that they are loved, and you will stand by their side no matter what. That is all we want to hear.

No one knew my pain but me. I was losing myself and felt like I was losing those around me. Life is funny. This breakdown was what I needed to clear the foundation in my life, so I could start rebuilding. I had to feel this loss, feel powerless, feel hopeless, in order to win.

CHAPTER SIXTEEN

My Comfort Zone

Mike and I were officially divorced. Tera and I moved back into my apartment. Mike took a lot of my belongings including my television, wine cabinet, and a Spanish portrait of the Last Supper, carved in white ivory, that I purchased overseas while on deployment. I was mad, but I figured if that was all he wanted after what just happened between us, then he could have it. I was starting to live a normal life. Tera and I had plenty of friends and attended many social gatherings. I was beginning to feel comfortable in my skin. Our weekend schedule was a repeat each week. Fridays were Rainbow Cactus nights where we watched drag shows and danced the night away. Saturdays, someone would have a house party, or we would go to Hershee Bar in Norfolk and then back to Rainbow Cactus on Sunday nights. I was having the time of my life. I was free and making up for all the time I lost trying to live my life "right."

I transferred to a new command, Aviation Intermediate Maintenance Department, Oceana in Virginia Beach, Virginia. It was a fresh start for me. I was studying for advancement to Petty Officer First Class or E6. I had a good working relationship with my co-workers. My happiness was climbing the charts again, or so it seemed. I still could not speak about Tera being my girlfriend, but it was okay. I became a master at making up titles for her. She was my roommate, my best friend, a girl that was my friend, my sister, a co-worker from the YMCA. It sucked, but I had no choice. Because no one could talk about being gay in the military, I never knew if anyone else was gay or not. I would watch people walk by to see if the males had a switch in their hips or see if the females walked in a masculine fashion. I would listen to conversations to see if anyone was speaking in code. Was their roommate a roommate or a significant other? All of us who were gay felt like we were the only ones, and because we couldn't talk about it, no one knew anything about anybody.

My LPO at AIMD was AZ1 Ben Mills. He was short, brown-skinned, very aggressive, but firm, and he smoked Newport Cigarettes. He was a jokester. He was easy to anger over situations he couldn't control, but as I grew to know him, I realized Ben was a very passionate individual about the Sailors he led. He did his best to take care of us. Everyone loved him. Ben was the very first person in the military I told about being gay.

"Aye, dog! Who the fuck you dating now?" he asked me one day when we were getting lunch on base at the golf course. He knew I was divorced but didn't know why. I still had my married last name, Greely, and I was in the process of changing it back to Kittrell.

"Why are you so nosey?" I asked, rolling my eyes at him. I knew I could trust him, but I wasn't going to give up the information that easily.

"Aye, man! I'm your boy! I'm just looking out for you. You keep talking about a roommate. I ain't stupid, man." he said with smart-ass look on his face.

"Her name is Tera," I told him reluctantly.

"Aw shit! For real? You serious?" he said excitedly.

AZ1 was so amazed. All I could think about was not wanting to answer 1,000 questions as to why I was with a woman. Heterosexuals always want to know why I prefer a woman over a man. The automatic assumption is that I hate men. No. I don't hate men. I am just not sexually attracted to a man. Mike could not turn me on. The first kiss I had with Tera did more for me than anyone could imagine. A common rebuttal is, "You haven't found the right man." Another issue with being gay is when people say I don't look gay. What the hell is that supposed to mean? I didn't know gay had a certain look. Think about someone telling you don't look black, you don't look white, you don't look Asian, Hispanic, or Mexican. Every race and culture has a mixture of people. Everyone does not fit into the same mold.

AZ1 Mills became my mentor, my friend, my big brother. He put the pieces of my life back together by allowing me to be myself and be open. I talked to him about every-thing in my relationship with Tera. He built that bridge of trust between us, and I was thankful. His being in my life as a mentor and counselor was a blessing sent from above.

One evening while I was at work, the office phone rang. It was AZ1 Mills.

"Aye, dog. What are you doing right now? You busy?" he asked.

"I'm working on log books. What's up?" I asked, confused as to why he was calling me.

"I'm headed your way. Got something to tell you," he said.

"Okay," I replied.

AZ1 walked into the office. "Come outside real fast."

What in the world could he want? He was scaring me.

"Aye, I just saw the advancement results. You made First Class," he said with a big-ass grin and a Newport hanging out of his mouth like an old southern black car mechanic.

"Shut the fuck up! No, I didn't!" I replied, not wanting to believe it. I did not study until two weeks before the exam. I was tired. I hadn't completely given up, but I was at a crossroads where bare minimum was good enough for me. I felt I had no reason to go above and beyond or even want to excel. I had no motivation. I did enough to just get by.

"Court, dog, you think I would come down here to lie to you?" He did have a point. "Don't say anything. You are going to get me in trouble. I just wanted to be the first one to congratulate you, homegirl! You made it!" AZ1 hugged me as I stood in total disbelief. Finally, there was a positive addition to my life, reinforcement. After taking the test six times, I wanted to give up. It was getting hard, but I was not in control of the roadmap of my life.

Making E6 is a big deal, and with it, comes more significant responsibilities. My joy was in knowing that I would not have to take another advancement exam for three years when I become eligible for Chief Petty Officer. It was my time to shine. I brushed off my shoulders and said, "I got this!"

I took over running the other AZs, working on F/A-18 Fighter Jet engine logbooks. I was responsible for signing and releasing the logbooks to squadrons so Fighter Pilots could fly and protect our nation. I was good at what I was doing. I was grooming and mentoring junior Sailors who worked for me. I developed a skill at motivating people and unlocking their potential. I could relate to their stressors and worries because I was going through stress and worry at the same time. They just didn't know it. My smile was still hiding my pain.

"AZ1, I'm getting ready to transfer to USS ENTERPRISE. The administration office needs an LPO when I leave. I'm putting your name in the hat to come run Admin," AZ1 Mills told me one day.

AZ1 was promoted to Chief Petty Officer and transferring very soon. I had never worked in an administrative office and knew nothing about it. I did not want to go somewhere not knowing what I was doing or how to do it, but Ben saw potential in me that I did not see in myself. The same way I was trying to unlock the potential in those I was leading, he was seeking to unlock the potential in me. I went to plead my case about not working in the administration office.

"Ma'am, I know Chief Mills talked to you about my coming to replace him in admin, but I don't want to leave the Engine Division. I love it down there. I love the Sailors, and if you move me, it might fall apart." I was trying my best to convince Lieutenant Commander Maxine Goodridge, but she was not having it.

LCDR Goodridge was a black woman. She was short in stature, wore her hair short and slicked down. She was in top shape. Her complexion was brown. She was very stern but fair. When she walked into a room, she never had to speak a word. Her presence was strong, and no one had to question if she was in charge. I loved walking with her in the mornings to get coffee. I felt a sense of pride and accomplishment. I felt motivated to do better and be better every day, no matter what I had going on. When she walked through the p-ways, she would part Sailors like the red sea. She was well known and highly respected.

"Chief, you better get her. I don't have time for this," LCDR Goodridge said as she walked away.

I stood there. I didn't know what to do or say. I just messed up. I was so torn. Why me? Why, out of all people, did I get selected to be in charge of all the administration needs of a 2,000-person command? I felt like I was not ready, but God said I was.

CHAPTER SEVENTEEN

My Testimony Pt 1

Reluctantly, I moved into the Admin Office. I had seven Sailors working for me. Quickly, I was thrown into the fire. The pressure of not making a mistake was real. I had never worked with awards, evaluations, naval messages, etc. All I knew was flight hours, man-hours, engine discrepancies, afterburner modules, and engine inspections. LCDR Goodridge made sure she provided plenty of course-correcting advice. I was terrified every time she called me to her office. I never knew what was found wrong on a piece of correspondence. She would hand me back the folder and tell me to fix it, but there wouldn't be anything circled or written indicating an error. I was to read and figure it out. I learned a lot from Ms. Goodridge by her doing that. Proofread everything before you turn in any document, mail any letter, or send an email. I made a vow always to take my time. Read and learn what it is that I am doing.

A couple of months after I took charge of the administration office, our command transitioned to new leadership. With that new leadership came new offices and new people. The entire way of business as we knew it changed. A new command, Fleet Readiness Center Mid-Atlantic, was established, and personnel was needed to move into the new offices and begin setting things up. Commander Joseph Rodriguez was taking over FRC. He was bringing his A-team to get the command started.

"AZ1, CDR Rodriguez wants you to move with him to FRC to help set up Admin," I was told.

"Set up Admin? What does that entail? I mean I am working admin now. I have finally learned the basics, but I'm not that good. Who am I leading? Will I have any Sailors?" I asked.

"Oh, you will have Sailors. About 2,000 of them, and civilians."

I could not believe what I was hearing. Again, I was selected to establish an entirely new office for a new command. I would oversee 2,000 Sailors and Marines in Virginia, D.C., South Carolina, Florida, Louisiana, and Texas. At this point, I learned to do it. Why not? There had to be a reason for this, and I knew in my heart that everything was going to work out for my good.

My new job was a demanding position. It was me and two female Sailors working for everyone else. It is a daunting task to be put in a leadership position to work with senior leaders who feel you are beneath them or who feel like you can't help them because of your rank. The military has a bad habit of looking at an individual's rank and using that to decide whether the person is smart or not. Rank has nothing to do with intelligence. A lot of the time you will find that young people have degrees and worked for a large business or ran their own business before enlisting. They have knowledge, skillsets, understanding and could probably teach one how to build a program using Microsoft Access. But leaders don't talk to their personnel to find out their true background. They make assumptions based on their rank.

I had to deal with this situation. Luckily, I had a very good chain of command who would step in and provide a little shift and rudder to support me and put the senior personnel in check. I was trusted in this position, so my only option was to give it my all.

I was on a new path in my career. Tera and I were still together. As I was moving up in life, I felt like she was not keeping up with me. I was being mentored by those who had gone before me to do better and be better than what I was. By this time, I had goals. I had ambitions. I had new standards. It wasn't that I did not love her. I was outgrowing her. People say that other people come into your life for a season or a reason. She was my season. I believe in my heart that I was in her life for a reason. She was not in school. She had a part-time job. She had no car. I did the cleaning, cooking, paying bills, and decision-making. We became more like roommates and associates in passing than two people in a committed relationship. She was subtracting more from my life than adding to it. I grew to want someone who could meet me at my level or provide more. She couldn't do that, and I could tell she lacked the motivation to try. I was an independent woman. I could do things for myself, thanks to having a strong mother as my first role model.

In July 2009, I owned two cars and bought my first house in Virginia Beach, Virginia. I was twenty-eight years old. I would never have thought I could have accomplished this much at such a young age. Tera and I moved into the house with the help of close friends. I was ecstatic. Things seemed to be getting better year after year—except in our relationship. By this time, we had been together for five years, and we had become detached from each other. We never went anywhere together. The excitement, the passion, the flames of desire were no longer there.

"I can't do this anymore," I said as I sat straight up in bed at 0200 in the morning. I needed to shed this dead skin so I could grow a newer, brighter, tougher one.

"What? What are you talking about?" Tera said, as she startled in her sleep.

"This. Us. You. Me. I can't do this anymore. We need to break up," I replied. My heart was racing. My palms were sweating. I didn't know what I was doing. I had no control over the words that flowed from my lips. It was as if a puppet master was manipulating me. I'd had enough. It took me four months to get to this point—four months to build up enough courage and mental strength to break away—four months to do it with no reservation, no worry, no stress.

Tera sat up next to me. I kept my head and eyes straight forward. I never looked at her.

"What am I supposed to do? I have nowhere to go. I'm not moving back home to Oregon," she said.

"I don't know what you are going to do, but right now, you need to move into the downstairs bedroom until you can figure it out," I responded.

It wasn't that I didn't care. I was done-done. People can tell you to break up with someone, but it's never that easy. We all have a friend who continues to say they are done with their significant other, but six months later, they are still together. A person will know when they are genuinely at the end of their rope. There will not be a second guess, hesitation, or a stuttering moment. The words will flow out, and you will surprise yourself along with the person you are breaking up with.

Tera moved into the downstairs bedroom. We agreed that she would be responsible for the utility bills as long as she was there. I was not providing a free ride. It was nothing personal, just business. I needed to focus on me and the work that was being done to put my life back together. I wasn't going to settle and be the sole breadwinner, enabling someone not to want better because I was providing for them.

While I was trying to fix my love life, God was fixing my entire life. Hindsight is always 20/20. He was preparing my table and inviting guests to eat with me that I would have never imagined. I was starting to understand and trust every mentorship session with those who took time to pour into me. He was writing my vision and making it plain. I stopped questioning why things were happening, why I was feeling so empowered, why my "dead" friends were falling off around me, why I was being favored. Instead of questioning and trying to figure out why, I started saying,

"I trust you" and made it a point that if I didn't understand what was happening, I would discover the lesson in the situation.

CHAPTER EIGHTEEN

My Testimony Pt 2

I was going about my daily work life as usual. I supervised two Sailors in all the administrative needs of the five commands we were in charge of. I quickly learned patience, obedience, what to entertain, and what not to entertain. I learned that people in leadership roles always feel entitled as if they are the only one in their rank. Some leaders develop a sense of arrogance and feel they should be treated a certain way and provided specific accommodations along with a spotlight. They forget how to be humble. They forget that they were once a "nobody" and someone helped them achieve their position. I did my best to hold my composure. I never wanted my Sailors to see me stressed out or angry. If I got worked up, then they would, in turn, develop a fear for no reason or feed off my attitude and become angry themselves. I never wanted that to happen. Having robust and calm leadership also helped. Command Master Chief Loran Mark Bather was my rock while I worked at FRC.

His demeanor was always calm, smooth, and collected. I never saw him get upset, become angry, or stressed out. He knew how to address a situation with the most professional manners. He spoke softly with his Caribbean accent, which made a person pay close attention to what he was saying. If he could hold it together, then so could I. He taught me that!

"AZ1 Kittrell, we have a meeting with Master Chief Woody this afternoon. Don't leave, please," said my Administration Officer, LCDR Erin Scott.

Oh God! What did I do? I thought.

"It's about your Sailor of the Year Board you did two days ago," she said. "You're not in trouble, silly girl." That was a plus. I could never tell what would happen with this job. As I said earlier, some leadership feel as though they are entitled to certain things and attention that I didn't have time for. I was respectful, but I knew the limits. I thought someone was in their feelings and reported me for something they felt I did wrong.

Around 1300, LCDR Scott and I walked into Master Chief Woody's office. He was sitting behind his desk, looking at his computer screen. My heart was racing, and my palms were sweating. I was genuinely stressed out trying to rationalize why I was summoned.

"Have a seat, AZ1," Master Chief said. I sat down slowly. My mind was racing. I looked at Mrs. Scott, and she gave me that closed, pinched-lip grin I had used myself at times. What the fuck?

"So, you had your Sailor of the Year Board on Tuesday, right?" Master Chief asked.

"Yes, Master Chief, I did," I answered.

Sailor of the Year Boards in the Navy is a recognition program for those who have done an outstanding job within the fiscal year. The Sailor's chain of command will submit a nomination package to the board members stating why a Sailor is deserving of the recognition. They start by nominating for Sailor of the Quarter Board, and at the end of the year, a Sailor is selected for the entire year. I was never interested in being recognized as a Sailor of the Quarter or Year. My thought was that I was there to do my job. I signed my life on the dotted line that I would protect and serve, that I would obey those above me, and embody the Navy's Core Values of Honor, Courage, and Commitment. I was never a spotlight person. However, unbeknownst to me, people were watching me from the bushes. They asked about me and what I was doing. The watched as I was moved from working on engine logbooks to working in the Administration Office, to establishing an entirely new command managing five subordinate commands. I was making moves and not looking back. I was outgrowing people around me and growing up professionally. I was finding my purpose and, thanks to Chief Ben Mills, I was getting snatched out of my comfort zone.

"Kittrell, I need your information for the Sailor of the Quarter Board next Tuesday," said Senior Chief Mark Farley.

"Sailor of the who?" I said shocked.

"You heard me. Get me your information so I can submit this package to the board," he responded.

"Senior Chief, really?" I said. "I don't want to do a Sailor of the Quarter Board. Besides, they already have their favorites picked out for the winner anyway. I don't want to waste my time."

Senior Chief Farley gave me that look. "You are not leaving work until I get what I asked for!"

"Okay, I will do it," I said. I was adamant that board members go through the motions of conducting boards to say they did it, but they already had their winner.

I finished my board on Tuesday and felt indifferent about it. No one ever knows what questions will be asked. Board members can ask a variety of questions from pivotal points in specific wars to access your military knowledge, to current policy and instruction changes, to opinionated thoughts. It's a coin toss. I didn't feel wrong about my board, but I didn't feel right either. I was just glad I made it through.

Now, here I sat in Master Chief Woody's office, with my admin officer, being questioned about the Sailor of the Year Board.

"How do you think you did, AZ1?" he asked me.

"I don't know. I feel like they already have their winner selected. I'm honored that Senior Chief Farley nominated me, but I'm good on that. I'm not stressed," I replied honestly.

"What do you think a Sailor of the Year should represent?" he continued.

"Well, a Sailor of the Year should be selected based upon their work, their leadership, their attitude, their professionalism, and if they lead by example," I answered.

"Really?" Master Chief asked, as he leaned back in his chair with his arms crossed.

"Yes," I replied. He just looked at me.

What the hell was this? I thought to myself. I felt like I was on another board but just one-on-one this time.

"Congratulations, AZ1," he shouted. "You have been selected for FRC Oceana's Sailor of the Year!"

I froze. I don't think I blinked for about twenty seconds.

"Wait. What?" I said. I could not believe it. I looked at LCDR Scott, who had not spoken a word the entire time.

"I knew all along. I didn't want to spoil the surprise," she said as she hugged me.

I was catatonic. Could this really be happening? No words could describe that moment. I was provided opportunities, and doors were opened for me. I walked through each of them as I questioned why. I was naturally scared of what I didn't know. But I still did what was asked of me because I knew there had to be a reason for it all. I went from not knowing what to do with my life or how to handle it, to dealing with personal pain and confusion, to hating who I was and why I had certain feelings, thinking that I would never be good enough, and that I was a failure. Now, I was the Sailor of the Year and ranked number one out of seventy other First Class Petty Officers.

God showed me who I was and what I was capable of doing. No matter the struggles, keep pressing forward. No matter the pain, keep running. When someone comes into your life, assess why they are there; a reason or a season. Listen to those who have set the course you are currently traveling. When they offer guidance and a helping hand, take it! You cannot learn how to be a successful doctor by talking to a taxi cab driver. Surround yourself with people who are where you want to be so they can show you how to get there. When people are falling off your friend list, and you don't know why, let them go. If you fight to keep them, you are blocking your blessings. I learned from T.D. Jakes that if you continue to hang with dead people, you will die. Don't let those around you kill you. If they are not adding positivity, wisdom, health, love, prosperity to your life, you don't need them.

Master Chief Ben Mills, Captain Goodridge, Captain (Ret) Rodriguez, Master Chief (Ret) Loran Mark Bather, and Senior Chief (Ret) Mark Farley were placed in my life to help me blossom during my season. They continued to pour into me. I will be forever grateful for them because they had no idea what I was going through, but they still managed to see something within me that I couldn't see myself.

CHAPTER NINETEEN

Aye, Aye Chief Pt 1

I n the Navy, Sailors rotate from sea duty to shore duty. Every rate or job has a different rotation cycle. In the aviation community, a young Sailor will graduate boot camp and spend their first four to five years on sea duty. Once they have completed their obligations, they will rotate to a shore command, where they will not have to go out to sea. Fleet Readiness Center Mid-Atlantic was my shore duty. I checked onboard, temporarily assigned, in 2005 and made my stay definite in 2006. I was there until it was time for me to rotate back to sea duty in February 2010.

"AZ1, I need you to come to ship and work for me, dog," said Chief Mills one day when he called to check on me.

"Come to the ship? And be ship's company? Hell naw," I replied. I don't know why Sailors hate being ship's company. Sailors who are stationed onboard ships, live, eat, and breathe there. From E1-E4, you live on the ship in compartments that contain anywhere from six to 300 racks (beds). Carriers are made to support the aviation community. When fighter jets and helicopters are not on the ship, the ship still has to maintain their certifications for the flight deck and all systems within the skin of the ship. All personnel onboard the ship have to keep their qualification in firefighting, damage control, flight operations, etc. so the ship will continuously go out to sea to conduct tests and certifications.

"AZ1, you need to come out here. It will help you make Chief. I promise. I need you to run the admin office for AIMD," he said.

"I don't know, Chief. I have been on deployments, but I have never thought about being stationed on a ship," I responded.

"Girl, get your shit together! You have done everything you need to do but this. You need to check this off your list so you can make Chief," he shouted.

Making Chief was a goal of mine. The Navy is the only branch of service that holds their E-7 through E-9 as a fraternity/sorority. To be a true Chief, you have to complete the six-week initiation process to earn your Chief anchors. They will never just be handed to a Sailor. Every young aspiring Sailor who wants to succeed in the Navy wants or has thought about earning the rank of Chief Petty Officer. The title of Chief, Senior Chief, and Master Chief brings with it, an entirely different level of respect from young Sailors, as well as from the officer ranks. Chiefs are the technical experts in their rating. They are the liaisons, protectors, leaders, parents, counselors, and sometimes only inspiration for their Sailors. Being a Chief comes with great weight. Only those who are genuinely ready earn their anchors and become a successful USN Chief.

"I'll call my detailer and see what is available for the ship. And I'll call you later today," I told Chief Mills.

I think I was about to make history calling to ask to go to a ship. Most females hate being on ships. Their way out of being detailed to a ship is to get pregnant, or they check onboard, and within six months, they become pregnant. A ship is not equipped for pregnancies, so females are sent most times to a shore base command where they can attend all their appointments. Now, just because a female gets pregnant and is removed from a ship, their sea duty obligations do not end. Once they have completed their baby leave and are fit for full duty, they will be screened to be sent back to sea to complete their sea time.

"Good morning! My name is AZ1 Courtney Kittrell. I'm coming up for orders soon to go back to sea duty. I was wondering if there were any billets for the USS ENTERPRISE," I said to my detailer. I could not believe I was doing this, but I couldn't not take Ben's advice. He set me up for greatness this far. I trusted him.

"You want to do what?" he asked me.

"I was wondering if there was a way that you could see if any billets were going to open up for ship's company on the USS ENTERPRISE," I repeated.

"You are asking me to do something I am not supposed to do. I will call you and let you know what I have. I can't just pencil you in for a billet," he said, and hung up the phone.

What the hell just happened? I thought. I was so damn angry! I was a single female, asking to be stationed onboard a ship, knowing I would have to complete two deployments back-to-back, and my detailer hung up on me. I went to my Chief upset about the situation. This was the first time I had ever called my detailer to negotiate orders, and this was my first impression.

"Chief Coram, I called my detailer to ask if any billets were coming up for the ENTERPRISE. He got mad, cursed me out, and hung up on me," I said.

"Are you serious? Naw...really? That don't sound right, AZ1. Did you call him back?" Chief asked me.

"Call him back for what?! That asshole hung up on me. He needs to call me back! I was trying to make his life easier by not having to beg, plead, and steal a female to go to a ship! Fuck him," I replied.

"AZ1" Chief Coram said, laughing at me, "Call him back and try to explain it again. I think he is having a bad morning. I can't see a detailer being mad because a female wants to go to a ship."

"I'll call him back, but not today," I said, as I walked out of the Chief's office.

I walked back to my office after going to get some coffee. I was calming down and was trying to rationalize why my detailer had an attitude. Maybe Chief was right. I mean, it was a Monday morning. Everybody hates Mondays. Then, my office phone rang.

"Good morning. FRC Mid-Atlantic. This is AZ1 Kittrell. How can I help you, ma'am or sir?" I answered.

"AZ1 Kittrell, this is your detailer. I apologize for earlier. I shouldn't have snapped at you the way I did. My morning has been rough. So, you said you were looking to go to the USS ENTERPRISE?" he said.

What just happened? Did my detailer call me back and apologize? Look at God! I sat back in my big black office chair, with my chest poked out, thinking, *you damned right*! But I kept my professionalism. When they go low, you must stay high!

"Thank you so much for calling me back. Yes, I was interested in knowing if you could tell me if any billets were going to be available for USS ENTERPRISE. My rotation date is January 2010," I told my detailer.

"Let's look at your record," he said.

He was reading through my evaluations and my awards. He looked at my Physical Fitness scores.

"We do have a billet that is opening up for an AZ1. I will pencil you in. When the billets pop open, I will send you hard copy orders," he said.

"Thank you so much! That is all I wanted. Also, I know you work in a customer service position, and it can be difficult dealing with people who think they are all that important. I can relate," I said. "However, you have to know when to flip the switch. What you had going on at work had nothing to do with me, but you took it out on me. I accept your apology. Just be mindful next time. Have a good day."

And with that, I was on my way to USS ENTERPRISE (CVN 65).

CHAPTER TWENTY

Aye, Aye Chief Pt 2

anuary 25, 2010, I checked onboard USS ENTERPRISE. I had been on naval carriers before, but this time, it was different. The smell of salty sea water with a stench of fish drowned my nostrils as I walked toward the ship. The ship was docked at Newport News Naval Shipyard undergoing routine maintenance and overhaul. The shipyard looked like a scene from an old steel factory movie with men walking around bundled up. It was a cold and rainy day. Smoke was rising out of the ground from the steam pipes, and birds were flying above against the gray, dreary sky.

"Chief! I'm down in the hangar bay. I have no idea where I'm going," I told Chief Mills. It was his idea for me to come work with him. I was not liking what I was seeing. So many Sailors walking quickly through the hangar focused on whatever task was given to them to complete. Pallets and boxes of stuff lined the hangar. Everyone was wearing white or baby blue hard hats because of all the construction that was taking place around the ship.

"Okay! Cool. I'll be down there in a minute," Chief said.

I waited, taking in everything I saw.

"Heeey Court! What's up? I'm so glad you're here. You don't even know," Chief said when he approached me. "I'll take you to the office so you can see where you work."

I walked behind Chief to my new office. It wasn't far at all from the quarterdeck where I entered the ship. that was quick and easy, I thought to myself.

We entered the tiny office. Three small desks lined against the right-hand wall. Behind the desks, were two more desks; one for Chief and one for the Leading Petty Officer, which was me.

"Aye, y'all! Stop what y'all doing for a second," said Chief Mills. "This here is my road dog, my ace! She is y'all's new LPO, and she will take care of you! Let her know if you need anything at all," he said.

Whoa, I thought. He is setting the bar high for me, and now I have to make sure I'm on point! The first mistake a leader can make is not to meet the expectations set for them. Young people are always watching those older, wiser, higher above them. They will never tell you, but they are watching. AZC Ben Mills set my bar high, and I accepted the challenge.

I settled in on board the ship and made new friends. I had a sponsor, Asabi Boatner, a black female First Class Petty Officer like me, who made sure I was comfortable and well-cared for. She introduced me to many other First Class Petty Officers that I would need to network with to get things done around the ship. I slept in a 324-man berthing.

There are unspoken rules when living in a berthing. The berthing is broken up into sections according to the different departments: Air Department, Supply Department, Admin Department, Combat Systems, Navigation, etc. You do not cross into another section unless you have been specifically directed to do so. It's almost like gangland. Respect those around you, and there will be no problems. If a female can't or won't give respect, she could come to her rack and find that someone urinated on her bedding. It's every woman for herself.

Before I arrived at the ship, I took the advancement exam for Chief Petty Officer. I was genuinely stressed out waiting to find out if I passed. The exam takes place in January, and results do not come out until March. Passing the exam or "getting your ticket to the dance" is like a rite of passage. You're not a Chief yet, but you have the chance to become one. Chief Petty Officers get excited to see who may be eligible. There are always jokes and funny threats about the initiation process. The Petty Officers are excited as well, but they are also scared. You see, CPO initiation is a six-week training process. Chiefs never discuss what it all entails. It is the real rite of passage for becoming a Chief. Those who never go through CPO initiation are shunned and pointed out. They are recognized as an E7 and never given the title of Chief Petty Officer. Junior Sailors know OF the process, but don't know THE process. They whisper and spread rumors about what they think happens. If they ask a Chief about initiation, the Chief will tell them, the only way to find out what goes on, is to advance to Chief Petty Officer.

"Are the results out yet?" I asked early one morning as I was walking in the office.

"They are supposed to be out today. You are gonna have to log onto your Bupers account to see if you were selected," Chief said.

"Ugh! Okay. I don't think I can look," I replied.

"Stop being so hard on yourself," Chief said. "You want me to look when you pull it up?"

"Yes please," I replied.

Work went as usual for the day. I was a nervous wreck! There was a time window when the results from our exam would post, but sometimes you don't know if its eastern time, central standard time, or mountain time, so you continually check all day! The F5 (reload) key on the computer became my best friend.

"AZ1, log in," Chief told me.

"Crap! Okay," I said. I logged into the computer. My heart was racing. My mouth was dry. This was a massive moment for me. Mom and I were starting to get back on good terms, and all I wanted was for her to be proud of her baby girl. I wanted to show her that I had my life under control.

As soon as I logged in, I turned my head as the webpage loaded. "Holy shit! You passed," Chief yelled.

"What? I did?" I yelled back.

I called my mom immediately and told her I passed my exam. I could not believe it. I could hear the excitement in her voice as well, and I knew she was proud of me. I was selected for Chief that year during the selection board process that takes place in June and July. The results from the selection board post in August. My world turned around instantly. The level of respect that comes with being a Chief Petty Officer is on another level.

As I mentioned before, a Navy Chief is like no other. We are the technical experts in our field. Big Navy knows that we understand and do our job, so we advance to every pay grade. At the Chief level, there is no more rate or job skill. We are now people managers. We lead by example, demonstrate professionalism, we are firm but fair, we adapt to change, maintain flexibility, and overcome adversity. These qualities are expectations of us at all times. I was now a black, lesbian, female Chief in the Navy. I had no idea what I was in for. Now and then, a wrench gets thrown your way that you have no answers for.

New Chiefs are always told that their first year will be like no other. They will encounter situations that can make or break them. They will be faced with adversity, pressure, stress. There will be times where you will not know where to turn for help in assisting a junior Sailor. Those words could never be truer.

My first pivotal moment as a Chief took place in February 2011, five months after being pinned. USS ENTERPRISE was conducting routine operations in the Middle East when we were directed to assist in a pirate hostage takeover. Somali pirates raided a yacht, the Quest, and were holding four adult hostages. All communication off the ship stopped. There was no email, phone lines, or the internet. Any connection to our families back home was non-existent. For two weeks, I watched as the Seal Team suited up and loaded into their assault crafts to negotiate with the terrorists to free the hostages. For two weeks, I thought about how the hostages had children and friends who loved them but may never see them again. The ship was in total lockdown.

Finally, one morning, Mass Casualty was announced throughout the ship. I knew then that we had rescued the hostages, but their lives were in danger. A Mass Casualty drill is practiced everywhere in the Navy. Assigned personnel conduct emergency first aid training procedures during different scenarios. The majority of the time, the staff doing the training are young innocent Sailors who may have never seen so much as a gunshot wound but are now training on amputating a leg or plugging a gaping sucking wound. They never in a million years think that one day it may be the real thing. It is always easy to practice and go through the same drills and routines, but when confronted with a real-life situation, everything that you trained for and practiced is forgotten because of fear and panic.

The four adults were brought onboard the ship. Three were already deceased, and one female was barely clinging to life. Young Sailors escorted her to the medical department where they tried their best to save her life, but she died too.

Anyone in a leadership position from the Commanding Officer down to the youngest Chief had to be strong for the Sailors onboard the ship during this time. So many questions asked and so many sleepless nights endured as we posted a 24-hour watch with the American flag draped over the cold storage unit in the hangar bay that stored their bodies. For those who witnessed firsthand the bodies and blood of the deceased, a lot of therapy was needed to overcome what they saw. As leaders, our job is to protect and take care of our Sailors.

We check on them to make sure their mental state is still good, to make sure they don't need anyone to talk to or that they are not contemplating suicide. A young Sailor told me, after the incident, with tears in her eyes, all she could do was stand there and cry when the elevator doors opened. She saw the older lady woman gurgling and gasping for air on the gurney, and she immediately thought about her grandmother and could not process what was happening. I wanted to cry with her, but I was trying to be strong for her. I told her that it was okay to cry, but I was talking to myself. This young woman would be scarred for life.

The death of the four Americans from the Quest will always be burned in my memory. I witnessed four deaths, two of them suicides, during my tour onboard USS ENTERPRISE. That was four deaths too many, but as military service members, we are taught to clean up the pieces and get back to work because we still have a mission to complete. There is not enough time allowed to process and grieve unless you do it on your off time. Not everyone adjusts well to traumatic events and needs individual counseling sessions to help them heal from the things they witness. So many Sailors separated from the Navy because they were unable to handle the pressures and stress that was placed on them with the expectation of not looking weak. Looking weak means, it's time for you to go home.

CHAPTER TWENTY-ONE

Blind Love

During my time onboard USS ENTERPRISE, I was a free spirit. Tera and I were no longer together on any terms. I was living my best life and meeting new people. I embraced all the attention I received when Sailors found out I was a lesbian. Not a lot of us were around. There was a time when no one would dare to speak of homosexuality because of the consequences that surrounded it. It was taboo.

When Sailors found out I was gay, the first thing they would tell me was, "You don't look gay." People seem shocked by me because I love my hair, makeup, high-heel shoes, purses, pretty nails, and flowy gowns. I do not walk around grabbing the crouch of my pants yelling, "Aye shawty!" Because I don't look all that intimidating, Sailors asked me for advice with their significant others or wanted to know how I came out of the closet. I told them it was not easy. I endured depression unbeknownst to others. I endured feeling like a failure because this lifestyle was not what my mother wanted, and I just wanted to make her proud. I endured worrying about losing friends and family, but I stood my ground. I learned to accept who I was and be comfortable in my skin. I have no control over other people's happiness, so their thoughts, opinions, and smart-ass remarks did not bother me. I live by six Fs that have come to be my motto: Fucking, Feeding, Financing, Family, First, and Fifteenth. If the people surrounding me do not contribute to any of these six Fs in my life, then they are irrelevant, and I move past them.

I learned to not use my sexuality as a way of thinking people don't like me. I owned who I was. First of all, it is never anyone's business who anyone loves or sleeps with, so I never bring it up in conversation unless I am correcting someone when they ask, "What does your husband do?" It was hard for me. It took a while for me to understand and walk with my head held high. Knowing who I am, and exuding confidence, diminished my sexuality from the thoughts and conversations of others. People accepted me for who I was. They were attracted to me due to my ownership and professionalism.

Trying to have a relationship as a Chief was difficult. I wasn't looking, but I would meet random females, and we would develop situationships. Once they found out what I did for a living, I guess it made them want to keep me around, but I didn't feel that at all. One day, my closest friend, Raquel, introduced me to a friend of hers. Raquel and I had been friends for eight years, so she knew my taste and my tolerance. I wasn't too keen on blind dates, but I gave in because I trusted her. The date's name was Princess, but all her friends called her P. Princess was light-skinned, tall, and athletically built. She loved and played basketball. She had long hair that she kept in a bun or bushy ponytail at the back of her head. She had the cutest, widest smile, with the prettiest, straightest teeth. She grabbed your attention because of her very innocent and childlike demeanor. She was cute.

"Aye, pimpin! I invited P over your house tonight so y'all can meet before we go to the club," Raquel told me.

"Really? You gave her my address?" I was annoyed but not really. I wanted to meet her as well.

"You good with that?" Raquel asked.

"Yeah, if she is already on her way," I responded.

The doorbell rang, and Raquel answered it. I sat on my couch sipping an alcoholic drink I'd made earlier. Princess walked around the corner to the living room from my foyer. She was something to look at. I was impressed.

"P, this is Court. Court, this is P," Raquel said.

"Hey! How are you? Make yourself at home. I have all types of liquor and juices if you want a drink," I told her as I shook her hand.

She smiled at me and said, "Okay, I'll check it out. Thanks." She walked into my kitchen.

I smiled at Raquel, and she hit me with the back of her hand on my chest and walked to the kitchen.

Princess and I dated for about two years. We shared the same friends, the same interests, and the same career motivation. I loved her, and she loved me. We took turns spending nights at each other's homes. I enjoyed our time together.

In 2012, I was selected to be stationed in Great Lakes, Illinois, as a Recruit Division Commander training boot camp. I was horrified! I had never been out of the state of Virginia. I was close enough to home in North Carolina, but still far away from where anyone would show up at my home unannounced. My cellphone rang from a number I didn't know. I usually don't answer unknown numbers, but for some reason, I answered this call.

"Chief Kittrell, I am calling because I saw an email with your name on it as a potential to push boots. I want to give you a heads up and see if that is something you want to do," said my detailer, AZCS Chuck Jones.

"Push boots? I just bought a house, and I'm returning from deployment! I haven't been home for a month yet." I tried to plead my case.

"Trust me. It will be the most rewarding experience of your life! I know how it feels to have just bought a house. I have a house I rent out in Chesapeake. I know the feeling! Girl, you are going to be all right," he told me. "You will be up for Senior Chief, and I guarantee you will make it by your second time."

"Can I wait until the reqs pop on CMSID?" I asked. I wanted to know what my other options were before I committed to moving to Illinois when there were orders to Hawaii.

"The only thing we have for orders this month is Whidbey Island, Washington, and China Lake, California," Chuck said.

"Shit! I guess I'm going to Great Lakes," I replied. All I could think about was my new relationship. What was P going to say about this? I could fly back and forth between Virginia and Illinois. We could both drive to meet halfway over long weekends. It could be doable. I had no choice in selecting for orders. Either way, I was moving out of state. Might as well take the closest state.

That evening, I called P as I usually did. We talked about our workdays, our families, and made plans for the weekend. I broke down and told her about the phone call with my detailer.

"So, my detailer called me and told me I was selected as a potential candidate to push boots," I said.

"Push boots? So, wait, you're moving to Chicago?" Princess replied.

"Yeah. I guess so," I responded.

There was silence on the phone. I knew she was not happy. I was trying to let her process the information.

"What's wrong?" I asked even though I knew.

"What do you mean what's wrong? You just up and took orders without even talking to me first. Now, you are leaving for how many years?" she said.

"I didn't have a choice. My only options were China Lake, California, and Whidbey Island, Washington. Either way, I was moving out of state. Talking to you would not affect my career. We are not married," I responded harshly. "We can make this work. I already started pricing flights and looking at distances where we can meet up over long holidays or fly in for the weekend. I'm willing to make this work," I told her.

I am a firm believer that people show you who they truly are when life gets complicated. If they are willing to stay by your side and put in the effort, no matter what, the love is real. If they have an issue or become angry and not even try to compromise, they never loved you from the beginning. At that moment, I knew in my heart, this relationship was over.

February 14, 2013, I took Princess and a couple of our friends to Washington, D.C. to celebrate her birthday. This occasion was hyped up for a month, and everyone was excited to hang out. Hindsight is always 20/20. There were signs of her not wanting to be around me, but I didn't see them. She was slowly pushing me away, but I was blind. I was so caught up in having fun and making sure her day was special. We stayed for the weekend in a hotel. There were two rooms that everyone slept in. Princess chose to sleep in a chair instead of in a bed beside me. I never thought about it. As everyone was preparing and getting dressed to go out to the club that night, Princess was nowhere near me. We never took pictures together. We were just never together. I wanted to ask what was wrong, but it wasn't the time or the place to have a falling out, especially during a birthday, so I held it in.

March 2013, we celebrated my birthday in Richmond, Virginia. It was a quick getaway with friends. Again, the same attitude was displayed between both of us. I was enjoying life, and Princess was acting very standoffish. Still, our night and my fun continued. I was not going to let anything ruin my birthday.

In April 2013, I returned from visiting my family. I called Princess to let her know I was in town and headed to her place to pick up my dog, Brownie. When I arrived at the house, I could instantly tell that she was in a bad mood. There was no greeting. No "I missed you." No "hey baby." Nothing. She walked into the house when she saw me coming.

"Your damn dog chewed my cords on the floor in the bedroom," she said as she walked away from me.

"Why did you leave her unattended in the bedroom, knowing she is a puppy and you have shit all over your floor?" I asked in a pissed-off tone.

Was she that mad? I knew there was way more going on with her than she wanted me to understand.

A woman's intuition is strong. We know when something is not right. People don't wake up and flip out for no reason. For every action, there is a reaction. I was on the reaction side to whatever Princess had going on. I wanted to stay and talk with my friends, but her nasty attitude told me that she did not care to be around me. I don't do drama, so I gathered my dog and went home.

I called Princess that night to find out what was bothering her. "I think we need just to be friends," She told me.

"What? Why?" I asked.

"It's not you. I have a lot going on right now, and I need space," she told me.

"Okay. I can respect that," I responded. Never did I ever think that Princess was cheating on me the entire time. I dedicated so much of my time and energy to her only to get disrespected at the end. Princess was seeing someone else for a couple of months behind my back and never told me. I found out through mutual friends, and my world was crushed.

Our breakup was rough. I never experienced someone so angry and nasty toward me the way she was. I would text her asking why she couldn't be honest with me from the beginning, but that led to her calling me names and telling me I was a fucked-up person. That was a pain I will never wish on anyone. She broke me and my heart and sent me to a deep, dark place in my life.

CHAPTER TWENTY-TWO

Rebuilding Who I Am

The breakup between Princess and me was very hostile. She was furious toward me and would not speak to me. People don't just change overnight for no reason. It always "takes one, to get over one." The summer of 2013 was a miserable time of my life. I was trying to hold together what was not meant to be. I now understand that I was being set up to receive greater than what I had, but I did not know that at the time. This one person truly blinded me. My trust, my love, my world shattered. As I scrolled through social media, pictures of Princess would pop up with the other female and the caption, "Finally in love."

In August of 2013, I moved to Gurnee, Illinois. I was in my fourteenth year in the Navy, and it was my first time moving out of Virginia and being so far and disconnected from home. My mother drove with me to help unpack and set up the house. It was a quick getaway for her considering she had never been to Chicago. I moved to a two-bedroom, two-bathroom apartment. Coming from a three-bedroom home, I had a lot of belongings. My apartment was a nice size. The complex was neatly manicured and offered a variety of floor plans along with garages for the heavy winter snow. I was in a new place, and I was feeling so alone.

Mom had to fly back to North Carolina, and I honestly didn't want her to leave. I had no idea how lonely and depressed I would become. I had a mutual friend who was staying in the same apartment complex as I was, but I didn't want to speak to her because she was a best friend of Princess's, and I didn't want to be around anything connected with her. I kept to myself, trying to process being in a new state away from family, away from friends I had made over the last fourteen years, and being okay with it. I struggled. The only person I wanted to talk to that could soothe me wanted nothing to do with me. I didn't want to burden anyone with my issues, so I kept everything to myself. Many nights, I cried myself to sleep wondering why I was being given these circumstances in my life at the time. I felt like I had lost everything; my love life, my family, and even my career because what I knew was no longer required for the job I was about to do.

Life is funny. It has a way of breaking you down to the core. Your world goes black, and you want to end it all. You think, who is going to miss me when I'm gone? I was broken to my core. During the Christmas holidays, I drove around my little town, looking at light displays on the houses in the community. It was the first Christmas I had ever missed with my family. I cried and spent the holiday alone.

I checked into Recruit Training Command in September 2013. Being a Recruit Division Commander was my most rewarding assignment. This command is where all Navy Sailors are trained with the fundamentals of Naval history, professionalism, military bearing, and respect. RTC trains all RDCs to be top notch and accept nothing less. We are humbly broken down professionally to help us understand how to educate our prospective recruits. I was privileged to train four divisions; two all-male divisions and two integrated divisions. I was advanced to Senior Chief Petty Officer and was pulled off push to be the Leading Chief Petty Officer for the scheduling office, and later, I was asked to take over Night of Arrivals at Bldg. 1301, better known as the "Golden Thirteen," where I completed my tour. Boot camp changed me as a leader. I never noticed until I was an RDC how much people look up to senior leaders. I would preach about it to my junior Sailors, but to physically see it every day, live it every day, and have recruits tell you, "I don't want to let you down," gave me a feeling that is indescribable.

My first division was a sponsored, all-male division, and all of my recruits came from Chicago, Indiana, and Wisconsin. I was a nervous wreck. I was responsible for changing eighty-eight souls from different walks of life to be better than the day before, to achieve a huge lifetime milestone, and be a part of something bigger than they were. I had an experienced RDC, AO1 Courtney Fletcher. This division was Petty Officer Fletcher's tenth division. I also had AM1 Brad Hill, who was on his second division with us. Being an RDC entails knowing how to motivate the recruits to come together and accomplish a goal as a team instead of as individuals. It takes a lot of work from the RDCs to make that happen. We have to know how to play off of each other in regard to our personalities. I was the mild-mannered individual, AO1 Fletcher was the "hugger," and AM1 Hill was the disciplinarian. It had to all balance out for the division to be successful.

With all the males in my division being mostly from inner-city Chicago, I did have fears of gang violence happening within the division or dealing with alpha domi-nant males who don't respect women. I did not know what I was going to get. Every Sunday, there was a team activity scheduled for the recruits in the division to learn about each other, which also helped the RDCs learn about the recruits. So many recruits come into the service after being homeless for years, being involved in gangs most of their teen years, and/or not having any role models in the family because mom and dad are locked up in prison. Some recruits' families disown them when they enter the service, leaving the recruit with no one to call home and no letters to read at night.

"On your feet!" I yelled as I walked out of the office, also referred to as the fishbowl.

"FFEETT!" the recruits yelled back. They were all standing at attention in front of their racks. I carried out a folded American flag.

"How many of you have folded a flag before?" I asked. Silence.

"Well, I am going to demonstrate folding this American flag with the help of another recruit. While we are folding this flag, I need someone to read this poem entitled 'Old Glory,'" I said.

Two recruits stepped out, and I handed one the poem, as the other recruit stood beside me. I unfolded the flag and instructed the recruit to hold the end of the flag tightly as I began to fold it.

"I am the flag of the United States of America. My name is Old Glory," the recruit began reading.

At the end of the poem and the final tuck and inspection of the flag, I stood in the middle of the compartment and looked at all the faces that surrounded me. Different ages, ethnicities, backgrounds, and religions. They were all here. Each with their own story to tell.

"I am going to pass the flag around. When it gets to you, I want you to tell me what this flag represents to you," I instructed.

"This flag represents my grandmother. She raised me and my brothers when my mom walked out on us. My grandmother died my senior year of high school. I never knew my dad, and I was left to take care of my younger brothers," said the first recruit. His eyes began to fill with tears. I could tell he wanted to burst out crying but was trying to hold it in.

"Pass the flag," I told him. Tears streamed down his face.

"This flag represents my dad, who served in the Navy. I want to be like him and become a Chief one day. He made sure our family was well taken care of. I just want him to be proud of me," said the next recruit. I made sure all of my recruits told their story. I did so to show them that no matter what block they repp'ed, no matter the color of their skin, no matter what state they were from, they were not alone. A smile can hide a lot. I knew for myself. I broke them down that day, and I was going to build them up over the next eight weeks.

It is our job to know where those we are leading come from. It is vital so that we understand what motivates them, what angers them, what their fears are, so that we can be able to relate. Without relating, there is no relationship whether personal or professional. It just won't work. After my first division, I made it my mission to know my recruits. I was getting them raw from the streets of their hometowns. A lot of them never had jobs before or even a driver's license. Their parents did everything for them, so folding their clothes and having to make their rack every morning was a struggle. I tasked my older, more mature recruits to be battle buddies with the junior recruits. I empowered the older recruits to be leaders and show the junior recruits how to study for the tests, how to make their racks, maintain their military bearing, and how to shave. When people are given a chance to show they can lead or are given an opportunity to be used to their maximum potential, they feel like a vital asset to a team. Therefore, they are motivated to continue working and accomplishing tasks because you trust them.

CHAPTER TWENTY-THREE

Trials and Tribulations

Recruit Training Command was indeed a test for me. The saying about RTC is that it can either make or break you. Meaning, you can stay strong and continue when circumstances are pressuring you to the max, or you can give in, give up, and lose everything. I saw it both ways. Some RDCs make this tour their most enjoyable, successful tour. They advance up to two paygrades higher or even earn a commission as a Naval Officer, despite the grueling working hours and time spent away from home and family. Other RDCs get caught under the power of the red rope and use it as a leadership bargaining tool: manipulating recruits and Petty Officers to do things against what is morally and ethically right. I witnessed RDCs get divorced because of infidelity and lose everything, including their Naval careers. RTC teaches lessons both personally and professionally.

"Senior Chief, um...you didn't pass the weigh-in," I was told when I had to weigh in to conduct my official Physical Fitness Assessment.

"Really?" I said, in shock. I never had a problem weighing in. I was fit. I taught spin classes and loved running up to five miles a day, and here I was. I failed my weigh-in.

"Wow. Okay," I said as the Chief guided me into his office. "Are you okay?" he genuinely asked me.

"Yeah, I'm fine." I said, but I wasn't. How was I supposed to lead my junior Sailors and get on them about their standards and responsibilities when I lost mine? I walked back to my office disappointed in myself. How could I let this happen?

"Don, do you have a minute?" I asked my Master Chief, FCCM Don Freeborn. I went straight to his office. I needed an ear to listen and make sure I wasn't losing my mind. I knew he would tell me if I was getting fat or if I messed up somewhere, somehow.

"I just failed my weigh-in." I told him.

"Are you fucking serious?" he replied in total disbelief. "What? How? All you eat is apples, bananas, and hummus!" He was correct. I was working at a desk, eight hours a day, five days a week. I went from marching all over base taking anywhere from 10,000 to 20,000 steps a day to sitting idly behind a desk. Some days, my legs would be so tired, I didn't want to drive home. I altered my eating. I didn't need to consume as many calories as before because I was not as active as before. I began eating more fruits and vegetables.

"I don't know. I don't know." I had nothing else to say. I was so bothered about failing as a leader. People were watching me. How dare I make a mistake?

I sat at my desk quietly. I tried to rationalize how I gained weight, even though I was working out. I wanted to make a medical appointment to see if anything was wrong with me. Having an answer would bring me closure, and the blame could be placed somewhere else besides me. I didn't want to take responsibility.

Later in the day, Don came to my desk. "How are you feeling?" he asked.

"I'm still in shock. Why? What's up?" I asked. I was getting the feeling that something was about to go down.

"If you could go anywhere on base to work, where would you go?" he asked.

"I would work at F.I.T. with the recruits who can't run or swim." I told him. "Why? What is this about?" I asked with butterflies in my stomach.

Fitness Improvement Training provides recruits who could not successfully pass their physical fitness test or their swim qualification with an opportunity to stay and continue working on it until they pass. Recruits are enrolled into the program after their division graduates boot camp. So, not only does a recruit attend boot camp for six to eight weeks, but they potentially might be there another six to eight weeks depending on whether they pass their run and/or swim test.

My thought process behind going to F.I.T. was to bounce back from my failure by using it as a positive instead of a negative. I now know the feeling of personal disappointment so now I could relate to the recruits who were experiencing the same emotions. As I try to motivate them and keep them focused and push them to achieve their goal, I would be simultaneously doing the same for myself.

"Well, I have to move you. I can't keep you as a Leading Chief Petty Officer if you failed the PFA weigh-ins. We have other Senior Chiefs who are doing everything they need to be doing and are looking for an LCPO position. Monday, I need you to check-in at F.I.T," Don said.

I could not believe what I was hearing. I got fired from my position. I was angry, but I understood. Two strikes so far in less than four hours, and the day wasn't going to get any easier.

I took a walk through the building to clear my mind. I wanted to go home and wish the day away. I passed Don in the hall. "Hey Courtney, also, we have to move you from the Sherriff Committee Chair position. You can still be on a committee, but you can't be the chairperson," he said.

Oh my God! The hits just kept on coming.

"Roger that," I said and walked away, trying not to tear up. I walked to the Career Counselor's Office, where my good friend, YNCS LaTricia Robinson, worked. I walked in, and she was talking to two other Senior Chiefs. All three of them were in charge of the Chief Initiation Season that year and were going over notes.

"Aye, Court!" she said as I walked in. I stood, looked at her, and my eyes flooded. She quickly ran to close her office door for privacy.

Tricia was a short, had caramel complexion, short curly hair, and very petite. She had been in the Navy twenty years and she was respected. She was an open and honest person. Very transparent. I loved talking to her because she had stern mannerisms and she meant business. Tricia could walk in a room and suck the oxygen out because you never knew who she was going to call out and correct or provide much needed input. She held me down while I was in Great Lakes. She was my big sister and still is to this day.

"What's wrong, booski?" she asked.

"I failed my weigh-in by 1 percent. I was just fired from Scheduling, and I have to check in at F.I.T. on Monday. I can't be the Chairman for the Sherriff's committee, and because I failed, I can't complete my Master Training Specialist qualification or register for my college classes," I said, crying.

"Oh damn, girl!" Tricia said.

"I want to sit in traffic," I sobbed. I felt like a failure. No matter how high up in the food chain a leader is, we all have a breaking point. We fight demons and battles inside us. The worst person you can disappoint is yourself.

"Naw, fuck that! Stop all that damn crying! Get your shit together, Courtney. Keep your head in these deckplates and do what you have to do. Now that you have a failure, you are going to be in the spotlight. Muthafuckas are going to be watching you! Keep grinding, girl. You already know what needs to get done. Stop feeling sorry for yourself," she told me. LaTricia was that one friend who gave it to me raw. She didn't sugarcoat anything. What she said, is what she said. I respected her for that 30-second talk. She changed my thought process that day and my life as a whole.

When negative things happen in our lives, we are so quick to throw in the towel, give up, and walk away. We refuse to find the lesson in our trials and tribulations. We are so stubborn that we miss out on our blessings.

When I worked in the scheduling office as the LCPO, I was the supervisor of one civilian guy, Mark, who was a retired Chief. Mark had been doing the scheduling job for more than ten years. So really, who was I in charge of? He taught me everything I knew. I had no Sailors who worked for me. It was just Mark and me. When I started working in F.I.T., I was not the LCPO, but I led twenty-three Sailors and about five Chiefs. Those who knew I moved from my LCPO position were upset and tried to voice their opinion on my behalf. I was grateful and honored that they cared, but to me, this move was a blessing in disguise. I didn't need a specific title or position to lead junior personnel. I just needed to be in a place where I could.

I led everyone in my new position and stood in for the LCPO, YNCS Jaime Jordon, when he was away. I held my ground and kept performing. I owned up to my failure and never made an excuse. I had to turn this around. I ran with the recruits three days a week when they conducted their fitness tests. I started working out, harder, on my own when I had time. I used my story of failure to motivate the recruits who were struggling with failure as well and starting to give up. People are always watching to see the next move. People take pleasure, for some strange reason, in the pain and failures of others. That is why people post videos of shootings, fights, arguments, car crashes, etc. on social media sites. Why do we glorify these things? Never give a person the satisfaction of them knowing you can't do it. Don't let them delight in your misfortune. During this time, I had two options: face everything and run or face everything and rise. I chose to face everything and rise!

CHAPTER TWENTY-FOUR

Face Everything and Rise

F. E. A. R.

"**C**ourtney! This is Don Garcia. Hey, I have a question. Can you pass a mock PFA when you get back from leave?" he asked.

"Sure can," I replied.

"Okay. I will let the PFA office know they need to do a fitness test on you when you return," Don said.

"Okay. Cool." I hung up the phone, confused about what had just happened. Why did he need me to complete a mock PFA? I didn't want to ask the question. I sat back and trusted the process God was taking me through. Obedience is the key.

I returned from leave and completed my mock PFA. I passed with flying colors. Nothing was told to me yet as to why I was asked to do it, so I continued with my regular daily schedules.

"Hey, Court, I just had a couple of the Master Chiefs ask me how you were doing working with me," Jaime said. YNCS Jaime Jordon was the LCPO of F.I.T., and he was my brother from another mother. Our working relationship was beautiful. I never had to worry if he had my back, and he never had to worry about me.

"That is weird. Don Garcia called me when I was on leave asking me if I could pass a mock PFA," I told Jaime. "What did you say about me?"

"I told them you were shit hot. You were making my life easier by stepping in and taking my meetings when I can't make them, and making sure that everything is being run right," he said. "Then they asked me if I would be mad if they took you away from me."

"What? Take me away to where?" I asked.

"I don't know. I think there is an opening for an LCPO position at Night of Arrivals. Don't quote me on that, though."

"But they are firing LCPOs right now for not having their MTS qualification. I don't have mine. I will be dink in February due to my failure. They know this, right? I have not kept anything a secret," I told Jaime.

"Yeah, they know. I don't know what is going on," he replied.

I was at a loss. If the LCPOs were getting removed like I was, why would they be looking for me to fill another LCPO position? I had two strikes: PFA failure and no Master Training Specialist qualification.

I was moved to building 1301, better known as "Golden Thirteen" to be the LCPO of Night of Arrivals. During my transition, I let it be known that I did not have my MTS qualification because I knew other LCPOs got fired for that same reason. Even though I did not have my qualification complete yet, I still studied my ass off. My thought process was that, if given the opportunity to take the test and do my board, I wanted to pass the first time up. I was not going to take for granted what was being done for me. I did not want to give anyone any reason to say, "I knew we shouldn't have chosen her!" It was my time to show my gratitude for the blessings that were being bestowed upon me.

November 2015, Command Master Chief Shawn "Izzy" Isbell, checked onboard as the new command CMC. He was a breath of fresh air. His personality was pure, and his stories were funny. Izzy was young. He was tall, bald, and very athletically built. He loved to work out, and his uniform looked like it was tailored just for him. He was a man's man. He welcomed all weightlifting challenges and told stories of old bar fights. I liked Izzy. He stopped me one day when I was in the main building and asked me to come to his office.

"Hey, I just wanted to touch base with you. I was told about your PFA failure. So, what happened? Where you injured? Couldn't work out?" he asked with concern.

"None of that. I just got fat. I own it. I wasn't hurt, I didn't have any surgeries, nothing. I went from walking miles a day to hardly walking at all, sitting behind a desk," I answered honestly.

"So, where are you at now?" he asked.

"I am the LCPO of Night of Arrivals right now. I am a little on edge because I don't have my MTS right now due to that failure and the other LCPOs getting fired for the same reason," I told Izzy.

"Why can you not get your MTS?" he asked.

"Because I have to pass two official PFAs before I can complete the qual. That means I have to wait until next summer to start up again. I will be past my due date for the qual," I told him. "I can't do anything right now. I tried to request a seat at the Senior Enlisted Academy, and I was told no. I can't register for my college classes, and I was removed from the Sherriff's committee as the chairperson."

"It sounds to me like all you want to do is be a Chief," Izzy replied. He was right. I just wanted to be a Chief. I didn't know what more needed to be taken from me for others to see that I was paying my dues.

The Navy loves to preach about resiliency, the bounce-back after a setback. Those of us who love what we do and recognize our faults do everything we can to be resilient. We look for ways to make up for our error. For me, becoming a part of the Command Fitness team would have been a way for me to bounce back. I didn't have that option at the time, so I chose to work with the recruits who were on hold and unable to graduate because they too failed their fitness tests. Being at F.I.T. gave me double pleasure. I was mentoring those just like me who thought it was the end of the world. I was also mentoring myself during the process, telling them what I wanted someone to say to me. Even though we strive to bounce back, a lot of the time our setback is held against us. It is used to set us apart when competing for awards or during the selection process for different boards. You never know how many times you will be kicked while you're already down, and they wonder why people give up and don't want to go on anymore or separate from the Navy altogether. Resiliency is preached, practiced, but never accepted.

February 2016 came, and I was delinquent in obtaining my MTS. My divisional LCPO kept me motivated to continue studying, and I did. Soon, I was told that the entire command MTS instruction was changed to reflect the passing of one official PFA, instead of having to pass two. My office phone and personal cellphone blew up with people cheering me on to do my test and board. I passed with flying colors. Later that year, I was selected, along with three other Senior Chiefs, to be a Chairman for the entire Chief Initiation season. I was so honored and humbled.

Despite the heavy seas, windstorms, lightning strikes, and rain, I held my head high and lived up to the Navy's core value of Integrity. That word carries so much weight. I could have walked away and run from my failures, but I didn't. I could have let it get the best of me and make me stop caring, but I didn't. I could have blamed everyone else for my mistake, but I didn't. I owned what was wrong and dedicated myself to fixing it. I can't lead others when I'm broken. I must always be and set the example. I assessed the situation and made corrections where they were needed, and people watched the entire time. My sister and one of my best friends, LaTricia, told me what I NEEDED to hear and not what I WANTED to hear. She made me pull my head out of my ass, get my shit together, and conquer what I had lost.

People are so scared of speaking the truth because they don't want to lose a friend or family member. If you can't be honest, then that person was NEVER your friend and is not considered family. Real people have nothing to gain when they are trying to stop you from falling off a cliff. Not only did I conquer all that I lost, but I was blessed abundantly more. I was able to attend the Senior Enlisted Academy, Class 201 Purple, which is a fantastic leadership course for all E-7 through E-9 located in Newport Rhode Island. I also completed two Associate Degrees as well. How you handle any situation in life will always define your character. It is only a failure when you fall and refuse to stand up.

CHAPTER TWENTY-FIVE

Power of Influence

The higher up a leader is in the food chain, the more influential they are. Some leaders make the best of it by being a pillar of quality, honesty, strength, integrity, dedication, and support. Some use it for their benefit and find themselves on the front of the Navy Times magazine, released from all their duties. Being an African-American female in a leadership role is not easy. There are not a lot of us around. Sailors relate mostly to those who look like them. Young black girls look up to those who look like them because a senior black female might be able to connect to their feelings, their needs, their stereotype. They see us as something they can achieve, even in a world predominantly filled with white males. Once the threshold of E-9 is crossed, the number of African-American females in the Navy is indeed smaller. There is so much we have to deal with. The pressure for us is not the same as our white female counterparts. AA females can expect to walk into a command already guilty of having an attitude, being a single mother with issues, not wanting to be a part of the team. It is unfortunate, but it is up to us to prove everyone wrong. It shouldn't be that way, but it is. In leadership positions, the pressure is even higher. We have the burden of not letting smart-ass racist comments bother us in an office of all-white males talking about politics, or the weight of not showing your ass and going off on another Chief in the workplace when you know he is doing something out of line, and it's affecting the Sailors. We are faced with the pressure of protecting a Sailor but trying to make it not seem as if you're only defending him because he is black. We deal with the stress of having to always be on point because young girls are watching, and we might be the only thing they have to look up to. Again, setting and being the example is a 24/7 responsibility. If we crack and lose our tempers, the young girls will think it is okay to snap back. Poise, grace, and a smile go a long way. Understanding what to entertain and what not to entertain is critical. It is not an overnight skill. If you keep giving clowns your attention, they will keep performing.

Fleet Master Chief (Retired) April Beldo, was an African-American woman in the Navy who held a very high-ranking position. Filled with grace and poise, she commanded a room when she walked in. Sailors loved her. Her career was ordained with career milestones and the first-to-ever-do-it stories. For the African-American females, she was a glimmer of hope that we too could achieve our dreams and be more than the stereotypes that branded us. African-American female Sailors adored her the most because of this, but she was overshadowed with the opinions from others that she catered only to black people. Sometimes, it's as if African Americans aren't allowed to enjoy the success and achievement of other African Americans because of perception from others. The PERCEPTION that we are only for us, when that is not the case. We embrace those to whom we can relate, those who bring a familiarity, and those who make us comfortable.

In June 2016, I was invited to be a participant at the Joint Women's Leadership Symposium that was held Washington, D.C. While there, Flt Beldo invited some of the female CPOs to her home for dinner. There was already a connection between some of us due to her visits to RTC. We enjoyed dinner, wine, and laughter. It felt like we were all lost cousins visiting from out of town. We were family. It was time away from work, and we enjoyed it. Flt Beldo asked for the gesture to be reciprocated when she came back to Great Lakes the following month, but because of work circumstances, we were not able to have another dinner.

In September 2016, Flt Beldo came to Great Lakes for a visit, and this time, we made dinner happen. I invited some of my friends, whom Flt Beldo already knew, to my house for dinner. All the women brought a covered dish of their favorite food and a bottle of wine. It was girl's night again, and we were looking forward to it. Music was playing, and laughter filled the air, selfie photos were being taken, and it was a pleasant evening.

"Courtney, do you mind if I post some of these pictures on Facebook?" Flt asked me. I don't usually share all my business on Facebook, and I wasn't going to share the pictures of that evening because of Flt Beldo's position in the Navy. I respected her, and I did not feel like having people asking me 1,000 questions or making comments about how or why we all were together.

"Fleet, It's your page. Go ahead," I responded. Deep down inside I wanted to say "Noooooooooo," but I can't be responsible for how other people feel. Fleet Beldo had about 5,000 friends across the Navy on Facebook. I knew the backlash was coming once those pictures were posted.

The next day, I walked into the drill hall for the morning PT session at 0500. All the newly selected Chief Petty Officers were lined up awaiting further instruction from the other season chairman and me. As I walked in, heads automatically turned and stared at me. I knew pretty much everyone saw the pictures from the night before. I kept my cool and kept walking.

"I would have loved to have dinner with Fleet Beldo," said one of the Master Chiefs.

"Well, you could have. You knew she was coming, right?" I responded, trying not to be an asshole, but it was too damn early for smart-ass remarks. Plus, I was pretty sure that the Master Chiefs knew Fleet Beldo was visiting the area. Why didn't they reach out to her on a Master Chief level and take her out to eat or welcome her to the city? They could have, but they didn't. She was their boss. PT commenced, and I began to swat away at comments being made all morning long.

Later that day, all the Chiefs gathered in the Chief's mess for training and to present going-away gifts to the Chiefs who were due to transfer from RTC. During this event, Izzy, as the CMC, held the meeting and provided direction. The Chiefs began to get loud with laughter, chatter, and moving around. It was bothering me because Izzy was trying to speak, yet no one was paying any attention.

"Aye! Shut the fuck up! Izzy is trying to talk," I yelled. It got very quiet and very still.

I looked back at Izzy, and I could tell he was frustrated.

"You know, all I ask is for common courtesy. Is that too much? Let me know. I don't disrespect any of you, and yet here I am trying to present gifts to our brothers and sisters who are leaving, and you can't even give me a little a respect," Izzy said. continued to talk, and it soon became a raging tangent about Fleet Master Chief Sue Whitman and her visit to RTC along with Fleet Master Chief April Beldo. He was upset that his leadership abilities were questioned when they both visited because they pointed out areas that needed improvement. There were things that we should have known from our CMC passing it through the Chief's Mess that we didn't know. I knew it bruised Izzy's ego a little, but he never said anything about it.

"...out of touch with goddamn reality! I know some of you in here are friends with Flt Beldo. You can go back and tell her what I said," Izzy shouted. I froze. What just happened and what did he say? I could not believe my ears. If Izzy had a problem with any of "US" being friends with Flt Beldo, then he should have come to us and spoken to us on another level. I took that tangent as an insult, and I was not going to let him get away with this.

"Izzy! Can I speak to you?" I said after our meeting, and everyone was leaving.

"Yeah what's up, Court?" he asked.

"Look, I don't know what just happened in there, but if you have an issue with us having dinner with Flt Beldo last night, you could have just talked to me about it. No one did anything intentionally to disrespect you if that is how you feel," I told him.

"You know, I saw those pictures on Facebook and said to myself, hmph, four out of five of those Chiefs belong to me," he replied. "Do you know how it made me feel when my Chiefs have a better reach to my boss than I do?"

"Izzy, no one was even thinking like that. I wasn't born a Chief yesterday. I have been doing this for quite a while. It was nothing but dinner with friends, and that was it. It wasn't like I was airing our dirty laundry at RTC!" I was upset. How could he think that anyone of us deliberately had dinner with "his boss" to disrespect him? I was appalled. After everything Izzy had done for me, allowed me to be Chief again after my failures, he would think I would betray him. My feelings were genuinely hurt. I left the building and headed back to my office. That moment put an awkward distance between us, and our friendship was never the same.

Later that day, I received a phone call from a number I didn't recognize. I was still thinking about Izzy's actions earlier that day. I know he meant no harm, but as a Command Master Chief and leader of our Chief's Mess, his power of influence was more significant than he knew. Having that outburst and temper tantrum showed the other Chiefs that it was all about him. He was upset that he didn't know? What would "knowing" about the dinner have done for him? Izzy had no control and was not in the spotlight with one-on-one time, receiving whatever accolades he thought he should have received from his boss.

"Hello?" I said.

"Senior Chief! What are you doing?" the voice replied. I immediately recognized it as Fleet Beldo.

"Nothing. I'm in the C school office bullshitting. What's up?" I asked.

"Call me when you get home," she said.

"Okay," I said, and I hung up. I froze, wanting to tell someone, anyone, that something was about to go down. It was very coincidental that she called after all that took place in the CPO Mess.

That evening, I called Fleet Beldo back. She had been informed that Izzy was upset about our dinner the previous evening. I didn't want to be in the middle of this stupid and unnecessary drama. I told her what happened, but I was still loyal to my CMC. Flt Beldo apologized to me. I told her it was not her fault. The picture taken at the dinner included five African-American Chiefs. That was the problem that stood out. No one ever has a problem with an image of all-Caucasian people in it. It is a typical sight to see everywhere you go, but the minute anyone outside of the Caucasian race decides to innocently do something together and not include one of them, it's a problem. It has always been and will continue to be like that.

Despite everything that was said and how he handled the situation, I stayed loyal. Honestly, I didn't want Fleet Beldo to fly Izzy to Washington, D.C., and for us to never see him again! He would never know how much I had his back even though he clearly showed he didn't trust me. The entire time Izzy thought I was spilling the tea on him and RTC, someone else made an anonymous phone call telling it all, and that someone wasn't me.

CHAPTER TWENTY-SIX

Unapologetically Favored

The incident between Izzy and me left me feeling uncomfortable. Different people would tell me that Izzy was explaining to everyone how "his Chiefs" had dinner with Flt Beldo, and we should have let him know. I was so over the entire thing and wanted to transfer quickly from Great Lakes, but I still had five months left to get through.

Military service can be ruthless. Every command you are stationed at, you begin to build friendships, relationships, and family connections with those you work with. Sometimes you have to weed out the negative ones, the ones you know are not adding any value to your life. Not only did I have LaTricia as a close friend, but I also had NCC Tongela Freeman, HMC Vicki King, and HMC Cassandra Townsend. No one ever knows why certain people are placed in our lives, but these three women changed my outlook on myself, empowered me to stand in my purpose, and never apologize for who I am.

"Courtney, are you coming to the going-away luncheon so we can give you your going-away gift?" a Chief asked me.

"Naw, I'm good. I don't want to be around Izzy. It will be too awkward," I replied.

That day, we had an event in the Chapel on base at RTC. All the Chiefs were leaving. Tongela, Cassandra, and I were still in the chapel talking and catching up because Tongela worked in another building, and we didn't get to see her often.

"Look, stop it right now!" Tongela said. "It's for your going away. Don't pay Izzy any mind. The situation is over and done with."

"I know, but deep down, it doesn't feel right. I don't want to be in his presence after the tantrum he threw. He can't even say anything nice right now, and he is supposed to get up and say some nice parting words about me?" I exclaimed. It had been a month since the "dinner," and there was still backlash from it. Izzy had not spoken to me anymore, and it was bothersome. I would rather not deal with drama or deal with someone being fake just to do their job.

"You are going to that luncheon," said Cassandra. Just then, Senior Chief Ponder walked into the sanctuary. I had never seen him before. He was a Religious Program Specialist and minister. He was new to the command. Tongela knew him through their community church events around North Chicago.

"Hey, brother," Tongela said. "Court, do you mind if I tell Rev your story and see what he thinks?" she asked me.

"I don't mind," I said.

Tongela began telling the story about our dinner. She along with Cassandra, Vicki, and LaTricia were there, so they knew what was going on. Rev slid his glasses off his face and started to look intensely at the ground. I could tell the story bothered him. I was waiting. I knew from the looks of it that he was about to either give me the business and tell me about myself or preach a sermon!

"Do you mind if I tell you a story real fast?" he asked me.

"Go ahead, Reverend," I said, not knowing where he was about to take me on his journey.

"Have you ever heard the story of Ruth?" he asked me.

"Aye!" shouted Tongela, who was an ordained minister. I turned around, and Cassandra was sliding out of her chair with both of her hands up, giving praise. What was happening?

"There was a field of women who were harvesting grain. Ruth and her mother-in-law, Naomi, would go to the field after the women were done working and pick up the grains that were left over. One day, King Boaz noticed her. He noticed how Ruth took care of and had the patience for her mother-in-law. More and more, he became attracted to her. He wanted to know who this young lady was. All the women were upset because they had been working in the fields forever and never had the King noticed any of them. They were upset," Rev explained to me.

"What does this have to do with me?" I asked. I was trying to correlate the story. I was raised in the church, but I wasn't raised-raised in church. So, this story I had never heard.

"Honey, favor isn't fair, and it's unapologetic. Are you mad because you have favor or are you mad because Izzy won't apologize for his actions toward you?" he asked me.

At that very moment, my life stood still. I had never thought that I was favored. I never thought about my life and how, when I should have been gone, I was still standing. I never thought about the people who were in my life that someway, somehow were mentors, protectors, and family to others. I never thought about how I was fortunate enough to know the people I knew or have the friends I had who supported me no matter what. I am who I am, and I should never have to feel bad or apologize for having favor. I am unapologetically favored!

That talk with Rev turned my mindset around. Never again will I feel sorry for being placed in certain situations at different points in my life that introduced me to people who molded and mentored me to be the person I am today. Those same people would become significant influencers in the Navy. I started to walk with my head held high and my chest out. I wasn't superwoman, but I wasn't weak either. My cup of green tea and incense could turn into a Black & Mild and Corona real quick! I could not be held responsible for another man's feelings. When God's blessing upon you start to irritate another man's demons, it is time to begin parting ways and focusing on you. I was, by no means, the perfect woman. I attend church, but I still curse a little. I don't go to church every Sunday, but I will blast gospel music in my car like a new Tupac album.

The day of the luncheon came. It was cold, and the sky was gray. I still didn't want to be a part of it, but my girls asked me, and I did it for them. There were seven Chiefs all together who were getting going-away gifts that day. The Chief's Mess at RTC contained approximately 250 Chiefs. Whenever there was an event, only about twenty to twenty-five showed up to support. It was usually the same faces, including Tongela, Cassandra, Vicky, and me. No matter what, we supported our mess brothers and sisters.

"Come on up, Chief!" Izzy said to one of the Chiefs who was leaving. "I don't know what to say about you. I don't think I have ever heard you speak two words, right?" Everyone laughed. "No, but seriously, you did your job well. I never heard anything about you, so you were doing what you were supposed to be doing, and that is training recruits. I thank you for that." Izzy finished up his parting words, presented the going-away gift, shook hands with that Chief, and sat back at the table. I was the very last name called.

"Courtney," Izzy yelled. Just then, his work cellphone rang. As I got up from the table, Cassandra and Tongela were clapping for me. They were my support system. I walked up in front of everyone waiting on Izzy's kind words and presentation of my gift. Izzy walked out of the restaurant on his phone. I stood there silently, while everyone stared at me. Was this happening? I knew I shouldn't have come in the first place.

"The Commanding Officer called Izzy about a file he needs. He had to step out," one of the Master Chiefs told me.

"Okay," I replied, still feeling awkward standing in front of everyone waiting for someone to say something. Then it happened.

"I'm going to speak," said Master Chief Garcia. "Courtney, there is no one like you. You have been an amazing addition to RTC and an amazing leader. No matter what challenges you faced and the failures you encountered, you never stopped going. You have bounced back from everything, and we all watched how you handled yourself. You are going to be truly missed!"

Another Chief jumped up. "Courtney, you have been a true friend to me, and I thank you! You never meet a stranger without making them feel like a part of your family. I'm going to miss you," he said.

"Courtney," said another Chief, "you have been my sister, my rock, and there for me when no one else was. You know my story and my struggles, and you still devoted time to help me. Thank you so much," she said, as she hugged me.

The Chiefs continued to speak one after another. I felt like I was in a twilight zone. It was surreal. Soon after everyone finished speaking, Izzy walked back in. I looked at him while holding the plaque that I was presented.

"Izzy," I said, "Do you have anything you want to say?"

"Nope," he replied. "I'm good."

I was shocked. Izzy spoke kind words for six chiefs before me. He talked about their careers, their children, their wives, their successes and had absolutely nothing to say for me. I walked back to my table where Tongela, Cassandra, and Vicky sat. They were all giving me funny looks.

"Did you see what just happened?" Tongela asked.

"She didn't get it," Cassandra said smartly.

"God intervened in your life and removed the evil," Tongela said.

"What?" I asked, confused.

"As soon as you got up, Izzy had to take a phone call. Everyone had nothing but nice things to say to you, how you impacted their lives. When they were done, Izzy walked back in and had nothing to say," Tongela told me.

I was in awe. I didn't think about it like that. Things happen for a reason. I was looking for acceptance and confirmation from the wrong person. I already had it from all the people who stood to tell how I impacted their lives. I was so blinded by the negative that I never saw the positive, but God showed me what I needed to see; that no matter what, I am unapologetically favored.

CHAPTER TWENTY-SEVEN

W hen I arrived in Gurnee, Illinois, it was my first time moving a long distance from home. I was stationed in Hampton Roads, Virginia for thirteen years before I moved. I recently bought a new house, made Chief, and was doing well with my career. However, my personal life was not so great. You see, being in a leadership position, you are watched by those who work for you. There is a great struggle with leaders trying to maintain the work-life balance because we are not trained to understand when WE need to get help. We spend the majority of our time mentoring, guiding, and parenting our junior Sailors through their pregnancies, divorces, breakups, court cases, domestic batteries, sicknesses, custody fights, and citizenships that we lose ourselves. We spend our days "raising" our Sailors. After dealing with Sailor issues all day, we still have to come home and face our own realities, divorces, custody battle, breakups, marriages, deaths, sicknesses, children, drugs, etc. that we have going on and no one knows about. We keep our business private because if we can handle our Sailor issues, then we can manage our personal affairs as well. No one stops to take care of us or notice that we are stressed out.

A lot of leaders have an alpha personality, so going to seek professional help means, to them, that they are weak. They can't handle life's small obstacles. They refuse to show emotion at work or ask for help. When they go home, they fall apart, trying to find ways to mask the pain, whether it's binge-drinking, drugs, or even suicide.

After Princess and I broke up, I was in an awful time in my life. I still was not comfortable talking about my personal life with my mother. She didn't have any disdain toward me, but I knew she wasn't comfortable and didn't fully understand my lifestyle, so I respected her by not inviting her into my personal life. I kept to myself, trying to find something to take my mind off of the hurt and pain I was going through. I would try to text Princess, wanting an explanation for our breakup, but it would only lead to her blaming me for everything.

A hit dog will bark. I believe that in a relationship, when one of the partners begins to act out of character, it is because they are guilty of lying, cheating, or stealing. The way for them to avoid being found out or being blamed is to act out by pushing the other partner away by any means necessary. This will, in turn, lead to what looks like a mutual breakup, but all the while, the guilty partner was already with someone else. You have to get under one to get over one.

Those days sent me into what I know now was a deep depression. My days held deafening silence and dark light. There were times I questioned my life, my entire existence on earth, and my purpose. I wondered why I always seemed to be letdown. I wanted to know why I was being punished. What had I done to deserve the pain and suffering that I was going through? I sat quietly in my bedroom thinking no one would notice or care if I killed myself right then. Those thoughts were due to feeling lonely, feeling like a failure, feeling unwanted, and not having anyone to vent to. I didn't want to be a burden anymore. I wanted the pain, the suffering, the loneliness, and the sense of failure to go away. I didn't want to die literally, I wanted the pain to die, I wanted the hurt and depression to die, but because it was all within me, the only way to get to it would be to go through me.

The only thing that kept me standing during the day was RDC school. No one knew my true mental state. No one knew the thoughts that possessed me when I was home alone with deafening silence. I was cheerful, happy, funny and outgoing at school. I was that one "strong" friend who appeared to have it all together. I was the class leader. I had people depending on me to answer questions, to lead them, to stand up for them. How could I be weak leading my people? I couldn't. That was not an option. Why would anyone feel the need to ask me, "How are you doing/feeling today?" If one person had asked me that question, I would have opened the floodgates and poured out my heart. It was what I needed and wanted but didn't know how to express. So, I stayed low, wore my happy mask every day during school, and made it through. I found comfort in being surrounded by others.

Having thoughts of suicide is something no one can explain. Two people fit this category. Those who talk about it and threaten it out loud are usually the ones who never go through with it. They are pleading for attention. Those who hold it all in without uttering one word are often the ones who are successful. They don't want to burden anyone and feel as though they will handle everything themselves without help, and it results in suicide. Family and friends all the say the same thing. "I don't understand. They had everything. They were successful. They were rich." Material things don't fill emotional voids. I could have had a million dollars, the fanciest clothes, the biggest house, and those thoughts would still have consumed me. I was grown enough at this point to look back on my life and see where my pain was coming from. It was arising from rejection, the fear of loss, and not being wanted. My father didn't want me, I lost my stepdad to cancer. I lost my grandmother and greatest friend, I lost my aunt, I lost a woman I thought loved me, and now I felt like I was losing my mind, as if I had no control. I was tired of suffering, and no amount of anything was going to fill that void in my life of emptiness in my soul.

In February 2014, I logged onto Facebook and was chatting with different female Chiefs in a group when I came across the profile picture of a woman I thought was beautiful. Her smile was so big and bright. She had the straightest teeth. Her skin was caramel, and her hair was very long and pulled into a braided ponytail. She was the highlight of the chat group. She would post funny, sometimes controversial comments or pictures that would send the other women in an uproar. I loved her sense of humor and wanted to know more about her. I began stalking her Facebook page to see her history and get a better feel of her personality and life. I saw that she was "family," and I was even more intrigued. Her name was Tiffany "Tiki" Rose Barber.

Tiffany was born and raised in Salisbury, North Carolina, forty-five minutes outside of Greensboro. She was a sporty chick, running track and playing football. Tiffany was more of an introvert than an extrovert. Although she loved to host parties, she didn't like to be around people. Growing up, Tiffany didn't have a lot of friends because she was very tomboyish and smarter than most kids. She was picked on for who she was. Her parents, Sharon and Avery, raised her to accept her flaws and be comfortable in her skin, so she was. I sent Tiffany a message one day after she made a controversial post in our group chat.

"Oh my God! You have those females mad as hell in the group. Lol!" I texted.

"Lol! They will be okay! Should I post this on there?" she texted back. It was a picture of a cake that read "Happy Sidechick Day!" It was February 15, 2014.

"Sure," I told her.

From that one message, Tiffany and I were inseparable. I was enamored. I couldn't believe that she responded to me. I was finally starting to smile again. I couldn't wait to come home in the evenings and hear about her work adventures and tell her about the crazy recruits I was training. She felt so familiar and easy for me. I was comfortable. The sun was starting to shine in my life.

At the time I met Tiffany online, she was stationed at White House Communications Agency in Washington, D.C. She was in charge of all communication setup and breakdown for President Barack Obama. She was responsible for setting up his speaking podium for his inauguration and his lights and flags on overseas trips. She was also in charge of securing his locations and inspecting local businesses and hospitals if they were needed. She had a big responsibility, but she still made time for me.

"Don't play with me! I'll fly to Chicago and come see you," she told me on the phone.

We would talk about who was going to take the first step to visit. I didn't think that Tiffany would, so I called her bluff.

"Stop playing. You ain't flying nowhere," I replied. The very next day, Tiffany found out she was coming to Chicago on a trip with Pres. Obama. She called me. I was happy and terrified at the same time. Did I bite off more than I could chew? Was I ready for all of this, or was I just using her as an emotional rebound because I wanted to feel like a had a purpose or belonging?

Tiffany arrived in Chicago. I arranged to meet her downtown at her hotel. We spent time together, and that was when I found out that she was going through a breakup of her own. She and her ex-girlfriend were at odds with each other, but Tiffany was trying to make it work. I felt played. After going through my breakup, dealing with some more bullshit was not on my agenda, and I wasn't going to stand for it. I gave Tiffany an ultimatum; it was me or her ex. I was done with games and heartbreaks. Done with dumb shit!

Months went by. Tiffany and I talked almost every single day. I would listen to her vent about her ex. I listened, as much as it pained me. I heard. I knew what it felt like to have emotion bottled up on the inside and not have an outlet. I was a living testimony to that. So, I was supportive during her struggle.

"I talked to my ex today," Tiffany told me as I was driving to work one day.

"Okay and..." I replied. I was shocked because this caught me off guard. Tiffany told me before that she was going to break it off with the ex, but it never came to fruition, but I still stood by her side. It was something about her that I didn't want to lose. I was upset on the outside that she was going back and forth, but deep down, I was going to stay through thick and thin. I knew she was the one I was supposed to end up with.

"I told her it was over. I didn't want to work anything out with her anymore. I'm moving on," she said.

"Tiffany, don't play with me. I am not falling for bullshit. I have been through too much, and I will cut you off," I shouted. But of course, I was screaming with excitement on the inside.

"I'm serious. I want only you," she said.

At that moment, I wanted to cry. It had been so long since someone voiced the slightest inkling of caring about me. It had been so long since I felt like I mattered or was important. All the weight and pain that I went through was lifted. The trials of life and confusion of relationships didn't matter to me anymore. I was happy that I went through the pain of Princess because had I not, I would have never met Tiffany or given her the time of day.

Tiffany came into my life when I could not get rid of a lingering black cloud. I had no joy or love in myself. There were so many sleepless nights when Tiffany and I talked about our dreams, goals, ambitions. She was headstrong and knew what she wanted in life. She was brilliant financially and very independent. For the first time in my life, I found someone who wanted to take care of me, rather than for me to take financial responsibility for them. I didn't know what to do with this newfound life. I was blessed at that moment. Tiffany and I married in 2015. The happiness and joy I have now cannot compare to anything. If I had to do it all over again—the pain, the thoughts, the loss, the hurt—I would, knowing that it would lead me back to where I stand today. Tiffany improved my confidence and changed my life. She made me a better person, and for her, I will always be thankful.

Sometimes we as people try to force what is not meant for us and wonder why things fall apart. A square peg will never fit in a round hole. We crave instant gratification. We want everything right now. When we do receive everything when we want it, we miss out on valuable life lessons. We miss out on growth opportunities. We miss out on understanding why what we have is valuable because we don't have anything to compare it to. We can't relate to the hurt and pain of a past situation because we never had it. We can't understand that the man or woman we have who cherishes and will lay down their life for us is so valuable because we never had anyone who didn't. When you have experienced loss and defeat, your gain and win is the most valuable thing you will ever have.

CHAPTER TWENTY-EIGHT

Sister, Sister Pt 1

Growing up I had two siblings, my brother Michael, Jr. and my stepsister, Alice. There was mumbling about my biological father having another daughter, but nothing was ever proven. I would ask my mother about it and she would tell me that my father did not have another child. I was his only baby. I grew up believing that. Besides, I loved my dad. Anything he told me I believed. He spent his time with me whenever he could. I was daddy's girl.

One day I received a message online from a young lady, Chasity Hairston. I knew of her because she, her sister Crystal, and I attended the same middle and high school. We spoke in passing, but nothing official, no hanging out together. Chasity was clearly upset in her message to me because she wanted to know if my father, Charles, was her dad. She explained to me that she was tired of having men DNA-tested to find her father. Her anger was directed at me and I understood why. I never responded to her message, but it made me think. First of all, that conversation should have been between her mother and my father. Coming at me was not going to solve her issue. I was not there when she was conceived. Second, I wanted my dad to just take the damn DNA test to get this idea, thought, notion over with and we could move on with our lives. It burned me up on the inside. If my dad says he is not the father, then why would he not take a DNA test?

November 2016, I received a missed phone call and a voicemail from my Grandma Ann. At this point in my life, it had been years since I had spoken with her. Why was she all of a sudden calling me?

"Courtney, this is Grandma. Call me back. It's about your dad. He is in the hospital and not doing well."

What? My heart dropped and at that very moment Uncle Tim called me. I started shaking.

"Hello?" I answered.

"Hey Niece. Look, your Aunt Phyliss and I are at the hospital with your dad and it's not looking good. We don't know if he is going to make it," Uncle Tim told me.

"At the hospital for what? What happened?" I asked nervously.

My Uncle Tim went on to explain that for two months my dad had been living with my Grandma. She was noticing that he was losing weight, but he would cover it up by wearing bulky clothing like sweats and thick sweaters. One day she went to my dad's room to check on him and he was lying in bed. He had lost so much weight that his body was a skeleton. He was weak and frail. Grandma called Uncle Tim and Aunt Phyliss to the house.

"Charles what are you doing?" Aunt Phyliss asked my dad.

"Dying," my dad replied.

I lost it at the moment. Despite not being a constant figure in my life when I needed and wanted him, he was my father. Without him, there would be no me. He did what he knew how to do, and I couldn't change the past. All I could do was try to move forward and hope for the best with our relationship.

Uncle Tim handed the phone to my dad.

"Hey baby girl," he said.

"Dad! What is going on with you?" I exclaimed.

"I am so sorry! I'm sick baby. The doctors are trying to figure out what is going on."

I'd never heard a grown man so weak in my life. His voice was low, harsh, and quavering. I could hear the pain of him thinking about the times that he should have been a better father but wasn't. I could hear the shame in him knowing that there was no excuse for the way he had lived his life.

When I hung up the phone, I sobbed uncontrollably. I wanted my father, but I didn't know at this time if I would ever see him again. Just one last smile, one last laugh, one more joke. I called Cassandra and Tongela. I needed support. Like extended family, they came over and prayed with me and sat with me as I vented and shared my pain. I will forever be grateful for them being by my side that night.

The next day I prepared for work as usual. Arrive at the gym no later than 0500, workout and be at work by 0800. It was rough not knowing the outcome of my father's illness. I received a message on Facebook from Chasity. She wanted to know all the medical conditions that ran in my family. My initial thought was *how dare you contact me when my father is about to die asking for family history!* My second thought was that she wanted a piece of the will if he were to die and we found out later that she indeed is my father's daughter. I do not remember responding to her messages. I was more bothered than anything else.

My Aunt Phyliss kept me updated on my dad's prognosis with phone calls every couple of hours. I was a nervous wreck. She told me he was going to have an exploratory operation because they found a large mass in his stomach and he could possibly have colon cancer. That was the reason for his shocking weight loss. My dad was unable to eat or have a bowel movement. Like most grown men, he despised going to the doctor. He would deal with things on his own. That mindset needs to shift. Not taking care of yourself is the most selfish thing you can do to your family. You would rather die than spend as much time on earth as possible. That is just another form of suicide.

The day my father went into surgery, I called every chance I got. Eventually, I became overwhelmed and decided to just drive to Greensboro from Chicago. It was a twelve-hour drive, but I did not care. I wanted to see my father because that would have been the last time. With the understanding and approval of my leadership, I left work, went home to change and pack a few items, and was on the highway by noon. I cried as I drove. I looked across the flat mid-western land and all of its beauty. I prayed for God to spare my dad's life. He isn't perfect and yet I still love him.

He isn't the most attentive father, but I will still support him. He has crushed me many times, but I still come back hoping that our relationship would get stronger. I thought about Chasity and how she must be tired and worn out trying to find the other half of her DNA. Not knowing who she belonged to. Being upset with me because she believed I had a great relationship with my father. Everything that glitters isn't gold. Even salt looks like sugar. I arrived at my Uncle Tim and Aunt Phyliss' house around 0100 Saturday morning. Aunt Phyliss made me her famous poo-poo platter; an appetizer tray with olives, crackers, cheese, meats, etc. Pairs well with a cold glass of wine.

Saturday morning after I slept for a couple of hours, we headed to the hospital to see my dad. It had been a couple of years since I had last seen him. He would call me on Sundays, and we would have Daddy-Daughter day watching TV shows together or televised track meets during the season. We would talk about life and he took a little interest in my Navy life, but nothing too heavy. As I walked into the hospital, I didn't want to excite him because he didn't know I was coming. My heart beat fast. My breathing became a little heavier. My anxiety was high. I didn't know what to expect with him lying in the hospital bed. The fear of the unknown was capturing and taking over all my emotions.

Dad was in the Intensive Care Unit. Surgery was complete and he was recovering in his bed. I had never seen him so frail as he laid in the bed. At one point he was a big guy, playing football, eating everything in sight and now he had the body of a weak twelve-year-old. His hospital gown engulfed him. The tubes running from his nose almost consumed his face. His arms looked like chicken bones with lose skin. His face was sunken in. His life was almost gone but his jovial personality and smart-ass mouth was still abundant. Dad's face lit up when he saw me. I smiled. I was glad that I was able to see him…alive.

We take our parents for granted until we realize that there will come a day when they will no longer be with us. We hold grudges and stay angry at things they have done to us that we felt were disrespectful and hurtful. Not everyone's story is the same. Some of us do have very evil parents and it is hard to have a relationship with them. In that case I say, there is someone in your life who "raised" you when your biological parent/s did not. Who are they? Invest in them and show them that you are grateful for their guidance, love, and loyalty. Family doesn't always mean blood.

My father healed quickly from his surgery. The diagnosis was that he had colon cancer and would require chemotherapy. Aunt Phyliss agreed to let my father stay with her and Uncle Tim. Since she was a registered nurse, she could better monitor my dad's medication and foods that he could and could not eat. In my head I knew that idea was going to be a rough decision. After a couple days in the hospital and the doctor's confusion on how my dad healed, they allowed him to discharge from the hospital and continue treatment at home. Home is where he went.

During the time that my father fell ill, he was let go from his job, he lost his apartment, but still had his car. He set up a GoFundMe account via social media to raise money for his bills. His old classmates and co-workers genuinely felt bad for him like any decent human being would for someone they know. They all donated what little bit of money they could. For some reason, I never donated money. There was something inside of me telling me not to waste my money. See, my father was taking the money donated and was buying marijuana to smoke. There is absolutely nothing wrong with that, but how about saving money and getting back on your feet. How about saving money and putting it toward helping around the house since you are eating everything without buying groceries, using power without paying a power bill, etc. I stood back and shook my head.

Here was a man that had 99 percent of his body in a grave, but for some reason God was not ready for him yet, so he blessed him with a new life. Dad spoke to mom and me in the hospital about wanting to be a family again, about how happy he was that we came to visit him and love on him. He was so sincere and genuine with the tears flowing down his cheeks. I thought, *Dad is gonna do right. He sees that he almost lost his life but was granted a second chance.* Little did I know, that nothing would change.

CHAPTER TWENTY-NINE

Sister, Sister Pt 2

I drove back to Chicago after my weekend stay in North Carolina. My heart was with my father. I prayed for his strength, his life, his health. I prayed for my aunt and uncle to get through their days with having another grown man in the house as if it were their child. I listened to all the gospel music I could on my drive through the mountains, looking at the majestic scenery. Then, I got a message from Chasity. *Here we go again*, I thought. I was definitely not in the mood to answer one thousand questions. I was not in a good space mentally to deal with my dad and her at the same time with different issues. I was frustrated. I wanted to lash out at my dad and tell him to just take the damn DNA test for Christ's sake! I ignored the message and continued with my drive home to the great state of Illinois.

In February 2017, it was time for me to leave Chicago and report to a new command in Virginia Beach. From November up to this point, I would call my dad and speak with him. Checking on him like he was my child that I dropped off to stay with family members. We had our normal conversations like our Daddy-Daughter days. It was comforting. But then he stopped answering the phone, so I called Uncle Tim to get check-ups on dad. He had a clean bill of health by now and the doctors were amazed that there was no detection of cancer anywhere in his body. I thought to myself, *they cannot be that stupid.* Marijuana is a true healer and my dad healed himself. By this time Tiffany and I were married, and she flew to Chicago to help me drive from the mid-west to the eastern shore. Halfway through our drive, we stopped at a gas station to refuel and eat.

"You hear about the results?" A message from Chasity came across my Facebook messenger.

I picked up my phone, confused and again, annoyed. Just then my phone rang.

"Courtney face! This is dad."

"Hey! How are you feeling?" I asked him.

"I'm feeling pretty good. What are you doing?"

"I am currently driving from Chicago back to Virginia. Tiffany and I just stopped to get some food and gas and we are now back on the highway," I explained.

"Oh. Right on, right on," He said in his famous joking voice.

"I have something to tell you. Remember Chasity?" he asked. How could I forget, I felt like I was the target of her anger because of my dad.

"She is your sister," he said nonchalantly.

Just then, I swear, Jesus took the wheel. I could feel my blood boil. What? When? Who tested who? When did this happen? Why didn't anyone talk to me? I had so many questions. I was ultimately in shock.

"Okay," was all I could muster.

I don't remember much of our conversation after that. I do remember being quiet for a while and thinking about Chasity. About how she had been fighting for so long to know who her father was. About how she was now going to want to know EVERYTHING about our family. About how there was just so much to say, and so much I wanted to apologize for. For my dad misleading her and not being tested years ago. How he had no regard when he knew there was a chance that I was not his only daughter. Here I was, thirty-six years and that is thirty-six years I missed having a little sister. Chasity had years of wanting to catch up with her dad that she never had. This was going to be an overwhelming situation. I was a bag of mixed emotions.

"Hey girl! Did your dad call you?" asked Aunt Phyliss. She called as soon as I finished speaking with my father.

"Yeah, he did," I said.

"How do you feel?" she asked in her nurturing way.

"I don't know. I am numb. It has not settled in yet. How did we go from Chasity is not your sister to, years later, now she is? What did I miss?" I asked in a monotone voice.

"Well Chasity reached out to me about having your dad do a home test. I told Charles he needs to get this over with because I was tired of hearing about it. He did the test a couple of weeks ago. The results came in the mail today. When I saw it, I ran upstairs to open the letter. It said he was ninety-nine percent the father. When I came downstairs to show your Uncle Tim, he walked out of the house," She explained.

Words could not express the feelings and thoughts that ran through my body and mind. After I knew about the results and finally made it home, I thought about calling Chasity and telling her about her new father. How not to expect anything from him. How he wasn't always going to be around. How he doesn't really check on you like a father should. I wanted her to know that the grass was not really green. There was no special relationship between my father and me. I just made the best of the little relationship we did have when I had the chance. I wanted to tell Chasity about Grandma Ann and how she could be a little ornery but meant well. I wanted to tell about our cousin Shaun who passed away in 2011 from HIV complications and was a beautiful human, our cousin Chagan who walked away from the family and we didn't know where he was or what he was doing. There was just so much. But I knew that wasn't my place. Chasity would have to reach out and ask questions to Dad, Aunt Phyliss, and Uncle Tim. I could not give her any answers because I did not want her to think that I was trying to sabotage her inclusion into the family. So, I stayed away and didn't speak to her. She had to find out for herself.

I went on a standard Navy deployment in March 2017. While I was away, plans were being made for Chasity to visit with Aunt Phyliss and Uncle and of course our father over the July fourth weekend. I saw pictures that were posted on social media. Chasity was married and had four beautiful children. They were all so happy with dad and grandpa. I could only imagine the questions she asked, and the curiosity about everyone in the family. It was a joyous occasion and I was finally coming to terms with everything. I was happy that the family mystery was ended.

When I returned home. I finally had enough healing time that allowed me to speak to my sister. It was then that I told her I stayed away because I wanted her to find out the truth about everything. I did not want it to feel as though I was mad, bitter, or trying to keep her away by telling her what was real. The real was not good. She continued to tell me that the July fourth celebration was awkward. Dad didn't talk much and wouldn't really answer questions. He was standoffish. I believed her. Dad went his entire adult life fighting the fact that he had another daughter. At the age of almost sixty, he had to bite off that stick and chew it. He was fighting the shame and embarrassment within himself. He didn't know how to cope with the situation. He was not prepared to face the truth of his actions. He was not prepared to answer hard questions about why he avoided ever talking to Chasity. I knew my dad was scared of what would come, but he would never speak on it.

Today, Chasity and I speak occasionally. I plan to visit her and her family one day in Las Vegas, Nevada where they live. She has had time to see and understand the truth of our family and how sparkles don't always mean diamonds. She doesn't have a relationship with dad. He stopped answering phone calls and responding to anyone. I haven't spoken to him since he called me about Chasity. We are both young, beautiful, black women with stellar careers and supporting spouses and he is missing out on the best thing a father could have. So many people have been through or are going through worse. Parents don't understand the pain and confusion that they can cause their children whether intentionally or unintentionally. It lasts a lifetime. It's not something that we just ever get over. I knew my father from the little time he spent coming in and out of my life. Chasity never knew her father and now that she knows him, she still does not know him.

If my father were to call me today, I would answer. If he were to fall ill again, I would drive home. If he told me he loved me, I would say, "I love you too!" To have that one last time is to have no regret later in life. Having a living father who is very capable of being a great father not wanting anything to do with their child is worse than not knowing who one's father is at all.

CHAPTER THIRTY

No one knows where their life is going to lead them. We are born into this world with our steps already ordered. We don't know what path we are to take. We grow up according to our teachings as young children and evolve the teachings into our own as we get older. We are expected to be decent human beings, treating others as we want to be treated. Leaders are not born; they are taught as well. Whether it's through life experiences or great mentorship, leaders are molded into what they become. I was taught through both life experiences and mentors. I will never be able to thank them enough.

As a black, lesbian female in the military, I struggled to feel like part of a family that is made up of predominantly white males. Racism still exists but will never be acknowledged because it's taboo. That is what I call invisible racism. There were times when I was automatically assumed to have an attitude because of the color of my skin, or I was made to look like I was an emotional wreck because I was female. Comments and actions are made around junior Sailors that are understood as racist, but no one calls it out. Sometimes junior Sailors feel they have no one to tell because no one will take them seriously. They will be made out to look, again, like they have an attitude problem and are playing the race card to get their way. It's sad, but they endure it. It happens more than we want to believe. Being a leader in my position makes the struggle twice as hard because I'm looked upon for help during these times, as an advocate to save the day. I shouldn't, nor should anyone for that matter, have to struggle with these situations in the workplace, but again, it happens. There have been situations that I have questioned: "If I were a white female, would I still be treated the same way?" I will never apologize for who I am.

Being a leader makes you a humble servant. You are charged with taking care of those under you through all matters good and bad. We are to serve them and their needs, but that leads to the question of, "Who is taking care of the leaders?" No one. It is up to us to recognize the need for a break. It is up to us to understand when we need to throw in the towel and say, "I need help," or "I can't do this by myself." But we don't. We try to be strong in front of everyone, so we don't seem weak, useless, scared, or unable to complete our duties. This is the recipe for all the alcohol problems, drug problems, divorces, domestic violence, and suicide issues within our leadership. They didn't know when or how to ask for help. They didn't know how to seek help, so they turned to self-medicating using one of these options.

I was asked by a fellow Chief at my command to help counsel a young Sailor who wasn't really a troublemaker but more of a nuisance. He didn't do anything egregious, but he did enough to draw negative attention to himself.

"Young man, where are you from?" I asked as he stood at attention in Service Dress Whites. I and two other Chief Petty Officers held a disciplinary counseling session with Airman White. We needed to course-correct him and provide him with feedback on how he was headed in the wrong direction.

"I am from Ohio, Senior Chief," he said.

"Okay. Did you live with your mother, father, grand-parents? Who raised you?" I always ask these questions to understand the person that is before me. A person's past can make them who they are today. If we don't understand the past, we definitely cannot understand the future.

"I lived with my dad, my younger brother and sister," he answered.

"Okay. Well, let me tell you something. There is some-thing about you that I don't like. Your aura is not sitting well with me. I don't know what you have going on in your life, but there is something you have not dealt with or you need to deal with. I need you to speak to someone today!" This was the first time I had ever spoken to this young Sailor. I had never had any interaction with him, but there was something about his eyes, his demeanor, that was bothering my spirit. He was twenty-eight years old and was doing things that a teenager would do. He was not a disrespectful kid. He did his job. He had never been in trouble before, but there was something about him that did not sit well with me.

During the time I was talking to Airman White, he began to tear up. I knew my feelings were spot on. I didn't care why he was in a counseling session; all I cared about was him getting help for whatever pain was trapped in his soul. He needed an outlet. He needed help.

Time moved along and all was quiet. Airman White was good to go until I received a phone call about him harassing a female at the barracks room on base. Airman White was drunk and decided to round up some friends to confront a young lady who he used to date. This young lady was also a part of our command. I assisted the Chief in dealing with the situation. Airman White amassed three federal charges that night; public intoxication, providing alcohol to a minor and obstruction. He was also given a direct order stay away from the female.

At the command, we held Airman White accountable for his actions. His chain of command supported the disciplinary actions and we moved forward. He was to attend an alcohol treatment program at the military hospital so he could better understand what was leading him to drink so much. The program was short-lived and they released him because he stopped complying with their orders. He came back to the command and because we felt he was a problem for the female, we sent him temporarily to another command while his legal processes were still being worked.

"Court! Ole, girl find you this morning?" Cole, Airman White's Chief, asked me as I walked into work.

"No. What's wrong? What happened?" I asked him very concerned.

"She was looking for you because she was on watch last night and Airman White showed up in the middle of the night saying he was sorry for what he put her through and if she didn't love him, he was going to kill himself."

I stood there in shock. What the hell is wrong with this guy? "Where the hell is he?

Find him and take his ass to the hospital. He wants to play this game; we will make sure we take care of him!" I told Cole.

Cole drove Airman White to the hospital for a psychological evaluation. They were there for nearly twelve hours. He was admitted to the hospital for a couple of days, but then again, he was released for failure to follow instructions and obey direct orders. Again, he was sent back to the command and we sent him to another command while we tried to figure out our next step and to keep him away from the female he continuously harassed.

I spoke with the young lady one day. I wanted to lay my eyes on her, to make sure she was okay. I told her that the Chiefs in the command were charged with taking care of Sailors. We are parents to our Sailors when their parents are not around. We are their protectors. If there was anything that I needed to know about, she should let me know. Don't try to handle everything in silence. Let me work for you.

She looked at me and said in her quiet, mousey voice, "I am good Senior Chief. Thank you. I can handle it. He doesn't scare me." And with that I smiled and said okay.

CHAPTER THIRTY-ONE

I was driving to work one morning in April 2019. Working hours for day check is 0700-1600. I usually arrived at work at 0700 or a little bit after. This morning was the same as any other. As I drove down Oceana Boulevard, my phone rang. I answered it through the Bluetooth in my car.

"Hello! Hey PS2!" I said. I saw her name on my phone when it rang.

"Senior! Whatever you do, don't come to work right now!" she screamed. I became instantly nervous.

"What do you mean don't come to work?" I asked.

"We have an active shooter. It's real! Its Airman White! He is outside shooting in the parking lot!"

At this time, I had just made it to the entry gate on base. All traffic had been stopped. Every emergency vehicle in Virginia Beach was speeding towards our base.

"WHERE THE FUCK IS AIRMAN JONES?" I yelled at PS2. I was shaking and tearing up at the same time. I knew Airman White was doing this to get to Airman Jones, the female he could not let go. All I kept saying in my head was, *Please don't let her be dead Jesus! Please!*

"I don't know how she is. I saw her on the ground and Airman White was on top of her. She had a black thing around her leg. He then jumped up and started shooting!"

I hung up the phone with PS2. I called another Chief from the command to confirm that it was indeed Airman White outside shooting. It was.

As a leader, there is nothing more painful than a Sailor being tragically hurt under your watch. The pain of not being able to rescue this young lady, who I just told I would protect, who was lying in the parking lot shot and not knowing if she was dead or alive, is this worst thing that I have EVER experienced. I wanted to leap, James Bond style, over every car roof and dive through the front gate to the command, scoop her up and fly her out of harm's way, but all I could do was cry and pray that she was okay.

My phone started blowing up with calls from friends who were hearing the story as local new coverage was beginning to take place across all news outlets. I called my wife and she was trying her best to calm me down, but there was nothing she or anyone could say at that point to make me feel better. I had no control. I watched as ambulances, police cars, forensic vehicles, and NCIS vehicles sped past all the waiting cars, wondering what was happening on their base. I was eventually told that the female survived because Airman White, for whatever reason, put a tourniquet on her leg. He told her he didn't want to kill her. He just wanted her to feel the pain that she caused him. I was in disbelief.

Did this really happen? I called my Command Master Chief for confirmation and he confirmed. When I asked about Airman White, he told me that Airman White was shot in the head and killed. The air in my body escaped.

Airman White was a son, a brother, a Sailor, a child. Now he was dead, in the parking lot at my command. How do we explain that to his father and his siblings? His family would have questions that we didn't have answers for. His family would blame the Navy for his death, when in reality we didn't know why he chose to end his life by a shootout with base police. Then there is the side that said, "Well he got what he deserved. He almost killed a young girl with no remorse." I was so torn and upset. I could not protect her. I could not protect him. We tried to get him help but we failed. No one ever saw this day coming. It was a dark day, but out of it came a bright light that Airman Jones did not die. Her worries and fears that she had tried to manage by herself were no longer. The command's struggle with trying to figure out how to deal with a Sailor who harassed another Sailor without being able transfer them was no more. But it left a mental and emotional scar on the Sailors who were walking into work that morning.

No one comes to work preparing an escape route just in case a co-worker decides to shoot at work. No one comes to work thinking about what they would do if someone was found lying in the parking lot from gunshot wounds, but that morning, that was exactly what happened. Grief counseling was held for our command through medical services. Our Sailors to this day are still attending regular appointments when needed. We do not know the true effect that the shooting had on our youngest kids. At work, it's easy because you are always busy with people and work. When they go home, we don't know how many reflect on that day and wish they could have done something to stop it. We don't know how many were close to being shot and/ or killed and had to run for their lives to get away. Some of these Sailors have never had an experience like this before in their life. They have never seen violence or dealt with stressful situations, but like every other day in the Navy, we suck it up buttercup.

That day will forever haunt me and my leadership. There has never been a day where I have felt weaker than ever. Felt like a failure. Thinking what else we could have done. What steps we missed. I lost sleep in waking up thinking about what the Sailors were going through. I become emotional thinking about why the hospital kept releasing Airman White. Maybe if they had kept him a little longer, he would have begun to open up, talk, and get the help he needed. He would not be dead at 28 years old. I can still see him walking around the command, quietly. I can still see the look in his eyes when I told him he needed to talk to someone to help resolve whatever issues he was dealing with. He is like a ghost in my mind that haunts me every day.

This is just one traumatic event out of many that I have endured in my Naval career. There are thousands of Sailors who have met similar experiences and are expected to carry out the mission the next day without a grieving period. This is one reason why I believe military members are "disconnected" from real-world emotions. We are taught to put our emotions and feelings in a locked box and move forward. This is why a lot of relationships fail at an alarming rate, because we can't relate to how others outside the military feel. Things that should be upsetting for anyone come across as no big deal to us. We don't cry or get as emotional as the next person. It's our normal and it's not normal. We all need counseling and therapy. We just don't realize it.

CHAPTER THIRTY-TWO

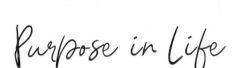

Purpose in Life

I n the beginning, I didn't know where the road paved for my life would take me. I didn't know that I would befriend amazing people and have them as lifetime friends. I didn't know the battles I would fight only to realize how weak I truly was. There was a purpose for my life, as there is for everyone's. I was just lucky enough not to question what I was receiving. All the rejections and losses I took on my path, made me a little more resilient each time. I trusted that everything would work out for my good, and it has. All because I held onto my faith. It is okay to try new things to see if they work for you. If they don't, it's not your calling.

We tend to want what everyone else has when they get it, but we are not on everyone else's timeline. A retired Master Chief, Kevin Doby, would always say, "You are delayed, not denied," and he was telling the truth. We have to stop trying to do what everyone else is doing and focus on ourselves. Our battles are not their battles. Our wins are not their wins. You don't know what they have been through to get where they are. You don't know how many times they were rejected or how many times they failed during their rise to the top. I have won battles that were for me, and I have lost battles that were not for me. The difference is that I understood the difference between the two. It hurt me and drove me into a depression, but God is not going to fail you. When you are placed in dark areas in your life, you are really being planted. Let those who care and love you water and fertilize you for your growth. You have to figure out how to grow so you don't die. I have faced rejection, been a target of jealousy, been doubted in my abilities to do my duties, I have suffered leadership failures, but it is how you handle the rocks being thrown at you that determines your character.

My journey has been an amazing ride that I would not change for anyone. I am still on my journey, trying to be the best example and role model I can be. I pray that my story motivates and inspires you to hold your head high, bask in confidence, and walk in your purpose. No one goes through trials and tribulations alone. There is always someone, somewhere, who has been or is going through what you are feeling. Reach out and ask for help. Call your family and friends and tell them you love them. Never let a day go by without a smile or a thank you for all you have been through. Every situation in life leads us to the moment where we are, and it's for a reason. Find that reason or lesson within and be a blessing to yourself or someone else.

There is nothing I would change about any of my stories. I have been blessed to overcome my feelings of doubt and despair, but I'm still working through some of my pain. This is my testimony. If I can make it through, you can too. I have been proud to call myself a LESBIAN, a WOMAN, and most of all a SAILOR in the United States Navy! I will always and forever be UNAPOLOGETICALLY FAVORED.

CPSIA information can be obtained
at www.ICGtesting.com
Printed in the USA
LVHW082102011119
635965LV00033B/407/P